Blessing of the Rainbow

Blessing
of the
Rainbow

First Edition: April 25, 2008
3rd print: May 24, 2008

Author l Norbert Dong-yeob Cha

Publisher l In-soon Baek
Publishing company l Wiz & Biz
Address l 426-7 Hapjeong-dong Mapo-gu Seoul, Korea
Tel l 02-322-1025
Website l www.fpi.or.kr
Publication registration l April 12, 2005 No. 313-2005-000070

Questions for purchase l 031-985-5677

ISBN 978-89-92825-28-3 03320
₩10,000

Blessing of the Rainbow

Norbert D.Y. C H A

Wis & Vis

There is a saying: "The consumer is always right."

The 500 thousand readers were right when they chose Blessing of the Rainbow.

Recently, readers have made a new request: "It would be so nice if you printed a compressed pocket-size version of Blessing of the Rainbow so that young people can enjoy it better. You see, I really want my children to read it."

I am sure readers are right about this too.

After much deliberation, I named it the "Smart Version". It is the English translation for 'something that is compressed and pocket-sized.' The Smart Version is an abridged edition of Blessing of the Rainbow that has dropped excess weight while retaining its essence.

I hope this will be good news for not just young people, but for all of you who are pressed for time.

NORBERT D.Y.C H A

What we need now is a holistic self improvement principle.

I have found that principle. It is hidden in "Shema Yisrael," which Jewish people who as an ethnical group have the highest number of Nobel laureates - must recite twice a day. Shema Yisrael teaches the attitude to approach a matter "with all your heart," "all your soul," "and all your strength". They teach this and tell their children to act on this "repeatedly". The secret to Jewish education, which has produced numerous accomplished world figures, lies in these four phrases.

"With all your heart(lev in Hebrew)" refers to emotional development.

"With all your soul(nephesh in Hebrew)" refers to will development.

"With all your strength(m'odekha in Hebrew)" refers to intelligence development.

"Repeat" refers to the aspects of repetition, persistence, and achievement in education(and training.)

These words literally constitute a holistic self improvement principle. Surprisingly, this principle corresponds with contemporary brain research studies that have established the functions of the human brain to be largely divided to the left brain, right brain, and corpus callosum, which are individual but also combined in their workings.

The "Blessing of the Rainbow," which is introduced in this book, has made this principle into a concrete system.(The outline appears in chapter 1 page 26.)

The "Blessing of the Rainbow" has three characteristics.

First, the "Blessing of the Rainbow" is a principle of hope.

Second, the "Blessing of the Rainbow" is made of seven practice rules.

Third, the "Blessing of the Rainbow" is a unifying principle that makes the whole into one.

I hope all young Korean parents, especially mothers, read this book and provide excellent education for their children.

I hope many good citizens read this book and instead of 'getting jealous when a cousin buys land,' they will spread a culture of congratulating one another, and enter into an era of 30 thousand dollar GNP.

Many people shared in the labor to create this book. I turn all recognition over to them. I also want to thank everyone who wrote reviews for this book. Thank you. Thank you. Thank you.

From my research institute in Gochon
NORBERT D.Y.C H A

| Contents |

I

The 2% that Makes a Professional

A professional isn't someone completely different from us.
They're only 2% different.

1 *They were different*

My Wish   I always speak of hope. During my television lectures, in my books, and when I meet people in person; I always speak of hope. Perhaps this is why so many people take a liking to me. A lot of people recognize me when I'm walking on the street, and among them a fair number come to me with pen and paper asking for my autograph. These individuals, I would like to call, are my fans.

This doesn't mean I pursue power and fame. To be truthful, I don't dislike either of these things, but by no means do I seek them. The thing I truly seek is "meaning". If something is meaningful, I carry out the deed with all my might. To me, power and fame are lacking in meaning and thus fail to attract me. On the contrary, I shun these entities because they cause feelings of guilt.

It was the world-famous psychologist, Viktor Franl, who compelled me to pursue meaning. Frankl established a theory through his numerous books that humans basically possess a "will to meaning". According to him, "meaning" is what ultimately makes human beings happy. Meeting him made me realize that the key to genuine happiness and success lies in the pursuit of "meaning".

What is meaning? I find meaning when I make another person happy, give hope to one in despair, console one who has been hurt, or help out people in need. Actually, real meaning is much larger than this, but even in these small acts there is meaning.

My wish is to succeed. I want to succeed. What is success? I will not say that such things as wealth, power, and fame are not "success". These things in themselves are conditions of success. Nonetheless, I will neither say that any of these constitute genuine success. True success must be something beyond that.

I hope that by reading this book, you will realize what this particular success is, and I also hope that you will soon become owner of this success.

THE JEWISH RULE TO SUCCESS

What if they were born in Korea?   Professor Moon Yong-rin, former Minister of the Ministry of Education in Korea, relates a very funny tale in his book, Intellectual Revolution.

Kim Ok-gyun(a prominent figure in Korean history who was an advocate of enlightenment) asked the great god to fulfill his wish. So, the great god said that if Kim Ok-gyun beat him in a game of Go, he would grant Ok-gyun's wish. Fortunately, Ok-gyun won.

"In our country, whether it is through their own doing or caused by others, many people don't know what they are good at or what they should do with their life. My wish is that three prodigies who have high potential to become paragons to the society be born in Korea."

The god pondered this for a moment and considering the unpopularity in the fields of science and technology, he had Einstein, Edison, and Marie Curie be born again in Korea. However, after several years, seeing that there was no development in Korea, the great god came down to examine what had gone wrong.

First, he met Einstein, who he found didn't even make it to college and was doing odd jobs. When the god asked Einstein the reason for this, Einstein explained that though he was most confident in mathematics, there was no way for him to get into college with just that single talent.

Next, the great god looked up Edison. 'Edison didn't go to college in his first life, so I'm sure he's doing fine,' the god thought, but to his dismay Edison was reading statute books in a closet of a room. The reason for this was Edison did invent many things, but it was so hard to get a patent that he was studying the patent laws in his room.

Lastly, when the great god met Marie Curie, this is what she said:

"No one would educate me or hire me because I'm a girl."

This story provides a small hint of what it takes to live a life where "everything goes well". It suggests what the lacking 2% is for us who crave happiness and success.

The difference between Jewish and Koreans   There are many leading world scholars, extraordinary artists, and people of great wealth among Jews.

Of the top 21 intellectuals who led the 20th century, 15 were Jews. Most of the prominent film directors and movie stars are Jewish, and half of the 40wealthiest people in the U.S. are Jews.

On examining the religion of 404 people who won the Nobel

Prize in Natural Science over the course of ninety years from 1901 to 1990, 76% was Christian, 22% was Jewish, 0.9% was Buddhist, and 0.1% was Muslim. This is a great accomplishment when we consider that Jews are a minority. In such a way, Jews distinguish themselves across all fields worldwide.

Then, how about Koreans?

The high intellect of Koreans has already been proven. At the end of 2003, Austria's University of Vienna Medical School compared the IQ of 50 nations, and the result showed that Korea ranked 2nd. In addition, according to PISA(Program for International Student Assessment), which is conducted by the OECD, Korean first-year high school students ranked number one in problem solving skills among 40 developed countries, corroborating Korea's strong intellectual abilities.

On top of that, Korea's high standard of education is, needless to say, top of the world. Koreans don't hesitate to be separated from their families if it is for the benefit of attaining better education.

Regardless, Korea cannot seem to produce worldly figures. People who are considered exceptional during high school become dimwits in college. This is the reality of Korean education.

How can we explain this? What is the difference between Koreans and Jews?

Sabra, symbol of Jewish tradition A word which embodies the Jewish childrearing method is "Sabra". Jewish people call their children, "Sabra," which is the name of a prickly cactus fruit. Their parents call them "Sabra" because the cactus blooms flowers and bears fruit in the harshest of desert conditions. Likewise, the people of Israel want their children to possess these qualities; to grow up strong and tough, and it is the tenacity of the plant that makes one appreciate the soft sweet interior of the fruit.

When they call their children "Sabra," this is what I believe is the message they are instilling in their children's minds:

"You are Sabra. My life was like a cactus. I took root in the desert and survived in the harshest conditions; without a drop of water under the blazing sun. I survived by drinking the few

drops of dew that would form in the dawn. Thus, how special you are. Before you came as my fruit, I had to endure years of pain and suffering. You are Sabra. My cactus fruit. Therefore, you must survive. When you do, you will bear fruit also. When you bear your fruit, call him 'Sabra'."

Israeli adolescents grow up hearing themselves called "Sabra" everyday. They are bound to be instilled with strong survival instincts.

Shema Yisrael; the Jewish rule to success   For Jews, the Talmud is where they receive their education. Though the Talmud is known to outsiders as simply a collection of allegories that contain humor and wisdom, infact it is a compilation that has been meticulously designed over the course of 1,000 years(B.C.500-A.D.500).

Dr. Tae-young Ryu, former professor of the National University of Israel, states in his book, The Fountain of Wisdom-What We Can Learn from the Talmud for Education of Our Children, that the Talmud is the very basis of Jewish education.

One of the most important spiritual assets in the Talmud is "Shema Yisrael(Hear, O Israel)." It derives from the Biblical passage in Deuteronomy Chapter 6, which all Jews must recite at least twice a day, at morning and evening. It is a pledge that they will live with all their hearts, all their souls, and all their strength.

"Love the Lord your God with all your heart, with all your soul, and with all your strength. […] Teach them to your children. […] ."(Deuteronomy 6:5.7)

The Hebrew word for "heart" is "lev," which means that we should use all our compassion. Hence, love God with our deepest affection.

The Hebrew word for "soul" is "nephesh," which means we must use all our spirit. In other words, love the Lord with our greatest determination.

Finally, the Hebrew term for "strength" is "m'odekha," which means that we must use our whole intellect. In short, we should love God with our entire mind.

These precepts give us the wisdom that creating good habits is the key to happiness and success. If we use all our hearts, all our souls, and all our strength in our daily lives and make this into a habit, then we will be able to achieve the best in any field we want whether it's in sports, the arts, education, or scientific research.

One thing we must bear in mind is the verse where it says we must repeat.Repeat! This refers to practicing, accumulating, and personalizing. Inshort, we must trainourselves by repeating again and again to make this into a lifestyle. We must impress those habits into ourbodies. Only then will we be able to wholly improve ourselves.

In my opinion, ShemaYisrael is the perfect model for human development. I will show readers the convenience of this principle through out this book, particularly in Chapter19 where I will reiterate and draw a concluding outline on the "Blessing of the Rainbow".

THE MISSING 2%: THE KEY TO SUCCESS

They used all their hearts   Charlie Chaplin worked at a steel mill before he became famous. One day his boss was too busy to go out, so he asked Chaplin to run an errand; buy some bread for him. It was evening when the boss was finally able to open the paper bag that Chaplin had brought, but to the man's surprise, there was a bottle of wine along with the bread. The boss asked Chaplin why this was so, and Chaplin replied, "Sir, you always drink wine after a day's work. I happened to notice that you're out of wine, so I bought both bread and wine for you."

Moved by Chaplin's thoughtfulness, the boss not only gave

Chaplin a raise, but changed the way he treated Chaplin from that day forth.

This anecdote sheds light upon Chaplin's secret to success that ensued as an actor. Chaplin was a man who knew how to use all his heart, even for things we might consider trivial. He had found the missing 2% that others lack. By using all his heart, he became one of the greatest comedians who ever lived.

They were positive thinkers   The 2002 Nobel Prize in Physics was awarded to Dr. Masatoshi Koshiba. That year, he was invited to deliver a commencement speech at the University of Tokyo. He had graduated from the University of Tokyo at the bottom of his class. During the address, he showed graduates his academic transcripts on a large screen, and of the 16 courses in his major, he only received two B's. The rest was even worse. Nonetheless, this man became a Nobel Laureate. What was his secret to success?

His secret lied in positive thinking. He called this "active cognizance," and pointed out that just because a person graduates top of his class, this does not mean this person will be top in society as well. On further discussing "active cognizance" and "passive cognizance," Koshiba claims that the value for "passive cognizance" is decreasing whereas the value for "active cognizance" is rising. He says that "passive cognizance" is where a person devotes to following in other people's footsteps. These people cannot make opportunities for themselves. Therefore, in order to become the best, we must use "active cognizance" and pave new roads for ourselves take the road not taken.

Masatoshi Koshiba was able to become a renowned figure in physics because he was a positive thinker who focused on what could be done instead of what can't be done. With this kind of faith, he had the power within himself to pursue new paths. He was a positive thinker who used all of his intellect to succeed.

Prepared to do the "lowest" work

This is a story about Kevin Roberts who is CEO of the worldwide idea company, Saatchi & Saatchi, which has offices in 82 countries and 7,000 employees.

In an interview with Mary Quant, a fashion house that was broadening its horizons internationally during the 1960's, Kevin Roberts made a proposal. He said he would work for six months at half the salary the previous employee had been working for. After six months, the company could pay him whatever amount they thought he was worth.

He was hired.

Roberts was prepared to start at the bottom. From the very start, he looked at life as an investment. Who would want to work for half the regular salary? However, Roberts considered his job as something worth learning, and took a shot at it.

Later, he reflects and says he loved every minute of it. "It was the passion, the inspiration and joy of those early Quant days, and that feeling still motivates me."

Kevin Roberts was able to succeed in the fast-paced ever-changing branding world because he had determination, even if it caused him loss in the immediate.

Didn't consider failure as failure   Edison said, "Genius is 1% inspiration, 99% perspiration." As you can see from this quote, he was a scientist who put extensive effort into his inventions. He had to fail 2000 times in order to invent the light bulb.

A reporter asked Edison how he felt when he had failed so many times, and Edison replied, "I didn't fail 2000 times to make a filament light bulb. I found 2000 ways not to make a carbon filament light bulb."

Edison never thought of his failures as failures. He merely considered "failure" to be "the previous step to success". In 1931, this great man left the world with over 1000 patents and through his efforts showed what true genus is.

Edison was able to become king of invention, and the 2%, which others lack but he had, was his persistence, which is the "Repeat" spirit of Shema Yisrael.

THE 7 LAWS WHERE ALL GOES WELL

About principles   There are rules in this world. There are laws. There are principles in life just as there are laws in nature. There are immutable laws that can be found in the things I have mentioned so far. A principle is when something occurs according to a formula, therefore, when you know the input you can predict what the output will be.

There are principles to success as well. We can succeed simply by satisfying the conditions to these principles. Similarly, there are principles to happiness.

We need a total self-improvement theory   All the
things I have mentioned so far The Talmud, Shema Yisrael,
and the missing 2% for success are all happiness and success
principles that are saturated inside the principles of the "Blessing of the Rainbow" that I am going to introduce to you.

As I was preparing to write this book, I read numerous
books on success and happiness, and while I generally
empathized with the books, I felt that there was still something missing. I was left with a thirst for something more
because most of those books only offered snippets of methods
or fragmentary prescriptions. This is why I nodded in agree-
ment while I read them, 'Yes, this will work!' but when I tried
to put those methods into actual use, I hit a brick wall.

Now, we need a unified principle.

Early on I realized that the Jewish Shema Yisrael of using
all your heart, all your soul, and all your strength, and that to
repeat this is the way to accomplish total self-improvement.
Then I became interested in the structure of the human brain
and human psychology.

Upon studying, I found that the human brain could be
largely divided into the Left Brain, the Right Brain, and the
Callous Body(the part in between), and that each part was
deeply related to intellect(reason), sensitivity, and will.

On the basis of this structure, each separate success principle and happiness principle was integrated into seven principles, which I call the "All Goes Well Theory" or the "Blessing of the Rainbow"(after the seven basic colors of the rainbow). Here is an overview of the principle.

Intelligence Development
(With All Your Strength: Left Brain)

Emotional Development
(With All Your Heart: Right Brain)

Will Development
(With All Your Soul: Corpus Callosum)

Personalizing
(Repeat: Overall Personality)

Blessing of the Rainbow 1
Think Positively
Blessing of the Rainbow 2
Scatter the Seed of Wisdom

Blessing of the Rainbow 3
Nurture a dream
Blessing of the Rainbow 4
Believe in Achieving

Blessing of the Rainbow 5
Discipline Your Language
Blessing of the Rainbow 6
Discipline Your Habits

Blessing of the Rainbow 7
Never Give Up

I have already passed on the "Blessing of the Rainbow" to many people; during lectures, consultations, and through my books. Using this principle, many individuals are already breaking free from what they once considered to be their fate. Practice this every day and you too can walk the road to happiness and success.

Happiness Guide

Make it a habit to use all your heart, all your soul, and all your strength. If you practice this, you will attain the best results in any field of endeavor. This is the final 2% to make you into a happy, successful person. Your opponent is yourself. Everyday you must make progress.

Use all my heart,
all my soul,
and all my strength!

📣 I can do it

1. Whatever it may be I will do it with all my heart, all my soul, and all my strength. This is where the key to happiness and success lies.
2. Emphasize my strengths. Make myself into a professional.
3. Find out what I like and take pleasure in it. Happy people are successful people.

In Order to Succeed, Be a Fool

Dr. Chang Kiryeo, a.k.a. the Korean Schweitzer, died at the age of 85, leaving a legacy of heartfelt stories.

One particular Lunar New Year, Chang's pupil woke up, quickly straightened out the blankets he had slept in, and bowed to his teacher in well-wishing respects for the New Year.

Dr. Chang gave a warm smile and offered words of wisdom for his beloved pupil. "This year, try living like me."

The pupil liked to tease his master fondly, so he asked, "I'd have to become a fool if I'm to live like you."

At this, Dr. Chang chuckled and said, "That's right. If you hear people call you a fool, then you've succeeded. Do you know how hard it is to live like a fool?"

People may have thought of Chang Kiryeo as a foolish person for offering free treatment to patients in need. They might have called him the "weird one" for giving out free food for the poor. However, Chang wasn't a fool. He was a person who had made a decision to live as a fool.

When Chunwon was hospitalized Chang was his resident doctor and Chunwon told Chang, "You're either a fool or a saint."

2 No Such Thing as Destiny

COMPLAINING ABOUT YOUR FORTUNE

A TV lecture episode   I recently gave a special eight-week lecture about the Blessing of the Rainbow on as how which is aired on national television. One of the episodes was based on the theme, "I make my fate" or in other words, 'there is no such thing as fate.' As I just said, I really believe there isn't such a thing as fate. I believe each and every person can develop their own destiny.

However, a funny incident occurred during this time. An astrologer wrote his opinion on the viewer bulletin board after watching this episode and the gist was this:

"Everyone is born with a destiny(a script or course to live by). [⋯] Fr. Cha was born with the fate to be a religious leader, which is why you are a priest now. Fr. Cha, if you want to know more about this science and about fate, please visit my research center. Because fortune is the most important science for everybody."

Could he be right? The answer is no. Of course, if you purport about a person's life journey, "This is your fate. This is the fate that is in your fortune," then that just may be your "fate". However, this kind of logic is a forced interpretation. If there is to be such thing as fate there has to be an undeniable law about it.

I don't believe in fatalism. If you look back through history there are numerous examples where great achievements were made with one's entire efforts in unanticipated circumstances and unexpected futures. Whether it is an individual or group, these cases have amassed into the world we live in today.

Proverbs on fate   Whenever something bad happens to us, we automatically complain of our ill fortune. Underneath this mentality is a strong belief in fatalism. We think, 'This is the fate I am stuck with.'

There is a common saying in the Korean language: "The

dog's life is the best life." This refers to times when you feel overwhelmed with much work and a dog's life looks enviable in comparison.

Some proverbs have spooky meanings: "You can hide in a pot, but your fate will find you."; "You can run as far as you want, but you can't run from your destiny." These proverbs are warnings that you should accept your destiny because you can never get away from it.

Moreover, there are proverbs that say, "You can deceive a tiger coming at you from behind, but you can't deceive your fate when it comes at you from up front." This is an extreme way of telling you that you can't control your fate.

Like this, there are many sayings we have lived with that tell us we cannot get away from what is destined. Consciously and subconsciously we live with the idea of 'fate' embedded in us.

Is There Such Thing As Fate?

A great enlightened monk   Is there such thing as fate? Li Yiwie expands on this question in the book, Three Inches of Tongue is Mightier than an Army of a Million.

Long ago, there lived a great enlightened monk. Many people came to ask about their fortunes, and among them were three bright scholars who were on their way to take the state examination. They were curious to know which one of them would pass the exam. After lighting some incense, they bowed in respect to the enlightened one. The monk gently closed his eyes and without a word thrust out one finger. Then, he shook a duster in the air and said, "Now go. You will know when it is time. I cannot reveal any more information, for it is of the profound secrets of nature."

The three scholars were curious to know more, but could only obey the monk's command.

After they left, an inquisitive servant asked the monk what the truth was. "Master, what did you mean when you lifted one finger in the air? Did you mean that one of the scholars would pass the exam?"

"That is so."

"What if two of them pass the exam?"

"Then, it means one of them will not pass."

"What if all three of them pass the exam?"

"In that case, it means not one will be left out and all will succeed."

At that moment, the servant understood the truth. "Ah… So this is the profound secret of nature."

King Seong-jong and a widow   Distrust in the 'four pillars' appears in an episode which dates back to the Chosun Dynasty.

A rumor reached the ears of King Seong-jong that a widow with the same 'pillars' as he was living in the castle. He summoned the widow to hear what her life had been like, and the widow told him the following.

The year Seong-jong had been named future king the woman's mother passed, and the year he had been crowned she lost her husband and was widowed. Therefore, every year a happy event occurred to Seong-jong, this woman had met

The same four pillars

adversity and now she was begging for food in order to survive. With everything she had gone through she concluded, "Never trust in the four pillars."

FATE CHANGES WHEN SELF-IMAGE CHANGES

Success depends on Self-image   Dr. Prescott Lecky, one of the leaders in self-image psychology, demonstrates how influential self-image is to one's life through the following research.

One student was failing in several subjects because of bad spelling. This student had misspelled 55 words out of a total of 100. The following year, the student got 91 correct and became top of the class by reestablising his image of self. Another student, who had quit school because she was doing so poorly, later went to Columbia University and became an honor student who got all A's. One boy's test results showed that the boy had no competence in English. The next year he won an award in literature.

These students hadn't been doing poorly because they were stupid. The problem was they had inappropriate images of themselves. They'd simply made assumptions after incidentally getting low scores in a test:

"I'm no good at math."

"I was never good at spelling from the start."

In short, they had paired their low scores with failure (Maxwell Maltz, Psycho-Cybernetics).

People tend to respond to things according to the self-image they have portrayed in their minds. A person who thinks, 'I can do it,' will eventually follow suit. A person who thinks, 'I can't,' won't.

The four-fingered pianist

Hee-ah Lee(1985–), known to us as the 'pianist with four fingers' was born with a congenital limb deformation. She has two fingers on each hand, and her legs are short stubs that do not exist below the thighs. Nonetheless, this did not stop her from becoming a pianist. Her trademark piece is Fantasie Impromptu by Chopin, an intricate piece that a person with ten fingers has difficulty mastering.

When Hee-ah Lee was seven-years-old, her parents decided to give her piano lessons because they thought it would help increase enough strength in her fingers for her to grip a pencil. At the time, even Hee-ah didn't know she would later perform on stage. What was it that made her into a pianist? In an interview with the monthly magazine, You, So Special(Issue Sept.2005), she said, "It was possible because

God wanted it."

When she was a little girl her parents showed her Bible videos and took time each day for gospel reflections. They knew it would be an arduous task for Hee-ah to play the piano, but they hoped for her to overcome her throes by accepting this as her cross. As a response to their faith, Hee-ah came to believe that God is with her wherever she goes, and with the strength from her firm conviction along with her strenuous efforts on the piano bench she has made her dream into her reality. She is truly a beautiful pianist who has changed her fate through her faith.

Happiness Guide

There is no such thing as fate. Fixation on fate will become your fate. Fate changes when self-image changes. Remove the old negative self-image and plan your future with a positive attitude. God helps those who help themselves. Make your own luck.

📢 I can do it

1. I will free myself from the fetters of 'fate'. I will make a new positive image of myself.
2. I will free myself from the thought, 'I can't do it.'
3. I will say, "I can do it!"; "Someone is helping me."

Tragedy of the Piranha

Piranhas are, as we all know, a carnivorous fish that inhabit the rivers of South America. In an experiment, scientists took these fish and put them into a tank. When the piranha had swum to one side of the tank to eat, researchers took a piece of glass and placed it at the middle of the tank, making a transparent wall. When the piranha were finished eating, they turned back and began to swim to the opposite side, but were obstructed from going further when they bumped into the glass barrier. The piranha butted their heads into the obstacle again and again trying to swim to the other side, but to no avail. After a certain amount of time, the piranha adapted and stopped swimming into the glass wall.

A few days later, the researchers took the glass wall away, but the piranha didn't swim freely like they had before the wall had been placed. They would swim to the middle of the tank and turn back of their own accord. If they were able to talk, they'd probably say, "This is the end. I can't go any farther!"

It goes the same for people. We can be just like the piranha and be hindered by our invisible walls. 'Me? That's out of my league.' 'That's too much for me to handle.' We've trained ourselves with these kinds of thoughts and we fear leaving our comfort zones.

Are you going to be the piranha in the fish tank, or are you going to be the piranha that swims free in the river?

3 *Success in the Brain*

THE BRAIN AND LIFE

Sweet respite   After I graduated from college I served
in the military in the Navy Officer Candidate School(OCS). I
received a 100-day intensive training course along with the
Navy and Marine Corps enlisted cadets, a training course that
is famous for its rigor, after which we would all receive com-
mission. I did quite well during the training period considering my small build, though I'm sure everyone has a tale to tell
of their experience in the military. Nonetheless, because of
my tall height, I always had to stand in the second-to-last or
third-to-last file because we had to arrange according to
height, but in the end I ranked 10th out of 150 Navy OCS's

who had come from the most prominent schools around the nation. This was an outstanding grade since I had received 0 points for gun shooting, meaning I had to make up for the lacking points in theory and physicaltraining.

I was nicknamed "Chadol(Korean word for 'quartz,' which also stands for 'a tough guy')" by my peers during the training period. This is wholly due to my utilizing the brain's power of imagination. Whenever there was a harsh exercise to endure, I went into my imaginary world and enjoyed the pleasures of "Utopia," and time would fly. I did rosary beads in my head during the 10km double march. Owing to this, I was oblivious to any difficulty. I remember I would carry a peer's rifle for him if he was having trouble keeping up.

It was the peak of training, which we called the "week of hell," a full week of no food, no sleep, and more intensive theory classes. During this time, we were not allowed to rest during the breaks between classes and had to undergo "full-jumping training". Full jumping training is the worst kind of torture when one is hungry and groggy. Our legs would just stick to the ground and wouldn't move. The instructors would each wave a baton about our legs so we couldn't help but jump unless we wanted to get hit by the rods. It got the men to jump even if it wasn't a "full jump".

I overcame this training through imagination. I imagined

that my body was as light as a feather and jumped like a mad man. I guess I was noticeable, because the instructor came to me and poked my stomach with his baton. I hollered my official rank and name.

"Cadet Cha, sir!"

"Repeat after me."

"Repeat, sir–!"

"Training state satisfactory."

"Training state satisfactory!"

"Take a break."

"Take a break!"

So, I alone was actually able to take a break during break time. It was a truly sweet respite. I must have looked despicable to the other cadets, but there were several other episodes like this during training, and this is all thanks to the power of imagination and mental strength.

In-brain Revolution   You can live a happy life if you apply the functions of your brain well. You are sure to succeed when you demonstrate the potential of your brain sufficiently. Furthermore, the brain is the key to your health.

The author of the book, In-brain Revolution, Shigeo Haruyama, studied the influence of the brain in great depth. He proved that 'what you think' doesn't stop as abstractide as in your head, but goes onto transform into specific substance and 'takes effect on the body.' As a result, head vocates the significance of positive thinking.

The brain secretes noradrenalin when a person gets angry or tense. Adrenaline is secreted when someone feels terror. When information of anger is transmitted from the brain to the body, the body goes into a guarded state and becomes a very tense(i.e. active) condition. Unfortunately, the substance which is developed in this condition is extremely toxic and so if a person gets angry or is stressed frequently, they are liable to get ill, or aging is accelerated and they will die that much sooner.

On the contrary, if you habitually smile and think positively, β-endorphins, which are beneficial hormones that activate brain cells, are secreted from the brain. This hormone not only keeps the body young, it also destroys cancer cells and makes people feel good. Therefore, if you want to live a long life full of joy and good health, without cancer or adult disease, you must live a life of positive thinking of which lots of good hormones are produced.

What does this mean? It means people's success and happiness lie in the brain. In other words, "in-brain revolution" will bring revolution to life.

Bringing Light To Mysteries Of The Brain

The future is in the brain   Brain research is the trend these days in Korea. Books that follow the latest fashion have spread its territory from business economics and psychology to brain science. International trends are just the same. The U.S. National Science Foundation (NSF) expound that the paradigm of science will go from the current info-communications to bio and nano technology and ultimately be fused into the fields of brain and cognitive science.

Why are people's interests leaning toward the brain? Is this because infinite potential is hidden inside the human brain? No, it's because the brain is everything to the human being. Therefore, research on the brain is in fact research about humans.

Structure of the brain   The brain is the starting point for all human actions, the conscious and subconscious. It is also the center for physiological processes, and the center for emotions and senses. In short, the brain is the greatest masterpiece created by God. It is the commander of noble ideas and creative activities made by humans. It's not only the core of human character, but the superintendent for all actions and emotions.

The brain is largely separated into three layers; the brain stem, the limbic system, and the cerebral cortex. The brain

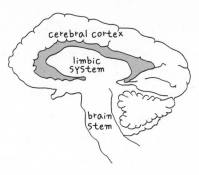

stem is located in the lowest part of the brain and is connected to the spinal cord, the limbic system is located above the brain stem, and the cerebral cortex is the part of brain that surrounds the whole limbic system and is also the largest of the three.

For reptiles, the brain mostly consists of the brain stem, which is in charge of the pulse, breathing, and digestion, so it is a matter of life and death if a problem in the brain should occur.

In the case of mammals, the limbic system, which controls emotion, desire, and impulse, is more highly developed than reptiles, and it creates the characteristics of what constitutes a mammal. The limbic system is in charge of appetite and sexual desire, which is a most necessary instinct for survival. The limbic system and cerebral cortex supervises instinct, which is very powerful.

The cerebral cortex which is a large part in the brains of primates has many wrinkles and consists of the frontal lobe in the front, the parietal lobe on the top, the occipital lobe on the back, and the temporal lobes on the sides. The cerebral cortex executes many things like deeply recognizing and speculating on the external world, and judging what comes first and last through law of causality. By having the cerebral cortex, we are able to have the abilities and qualities of human beings.

However, the cerebral cortex, the limbic system, and the brain stem are not independent entities. Whenever the cerebral cortex operates, so does the limbic system and brain stem. Therefore, the instincts that humans have are not the same as those of other animals. Our instincts receive workings of a highly developed cerebral cortex, guidance from our intellect.

Difference between chimpanzees and humans   The map of gene information which constructs humans, i.e. DNA, has an inseparable relationship with the brain. The structure of DNA is said to be 98.7% alike for humans and chimpanzees, meaning we and they are only 1.3% different. However, this small difference is in fact very big. The number '1.3' distinguishes us from humans and animals. It is because of this 1.3% difference that humans watch chimpanzees behind bars in their cages at zoos while the chimps are the ones looking out at us.

When people don't behave humanlike, it is because they are not well displaying the functions of this 1.3%. If you develop this 1.3%, you will become a refined human being.

This fact inspires our lives. Whatever we do, we will automatically be changed 100% if we transform just 1.3% of ourselves. This means that if you change just 1.3% of your 24 hour day, i.e. change your behavior for 20 minutes of your day, your whole life will change.

Left Brain, Right Brain, and the Corpus Callosum   The human brain is also separated by the Left Brain and Right Brain. These hemispheres, which are separated into two, differ not only in size, but by their functions and the hormones they produce. The right hemisphere controls the left side of the body and the left hemisphere regulates the right. Correspondence between the two hemispheres is accomplished through a chord of nerve fibers called the Corpus Callosum.

Generally, the Left Brain dictates linguistic, mathematical, analytical, logical, and rational fields, meaning the Left Brain is good at logical thinking and is competent in cognition of numbers and symbols, reading and writing, and calculating.

On the other hand, the Right Brain dictates non-linguistic, time and spatial, intuitive, and sensitive areas. The Right Brain is in charge of space recognition, and comprehending sight information. It is especially strong in the emotional like music and art.

Whereas thought in the Left Brain is orderly, it takes time in order to make decisions, so in urgent situations the decision is made by the Right Brain, which is intuitive and instantaneous.

In spite of these specializations, the Right and Left Brains function as a single-unit operation. This is because information is exchanged between the Right and Left Hemispheres through the Corpus Callosum.

It is important to develop a balanced brain. Since it is you who determines what will be input into your brain, you are the one to ultimately create your brain.

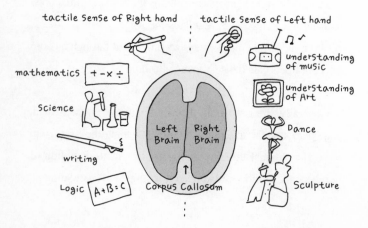

THE BRAIN IS THE KEY

The brain which regulates the human mind has a nerve called the A10. This nerve is also referred to as the "pleasure nerve," and when this nerve is stimulated, it delivers pleasure to us. But the interesting thing is since this nerve is connected as far as the frontal lobe of the cerebral cortex, it dictates from the highly primitive like sexual desires, appetite, and body temperature to the refined like exercise, learning, and memory.

This correlates to Abraham H. Maslow's "hierarchy of needs". He distinguished human needs largely into five parts: (1)Physiological, (2)Safety, (3)Love/Belonging, (4)Esteem, (5)Self-actualization.

These five needs rise in the form of a pyramid, from a lower level of desire to gradually higher levels of needs.

If a person lingers in fulfilling the lower levels of physiological, safety, and love/belonging needs, it is the same as being reptiles that follow the instructions of the brain stem or mammals that follow the instructions of the limbic system. Of course, the A10 nerve is also connected even to these parts of the brain.

However, it is when humans go a step further and try to fulfill their need for esteem(fame, respect), and need for self-actualization that we feel a higher level of pleasure. This is when the A10 nerve arrives at the "peak experience". Maslow refers to the state when a person's need for self-actualization is realized and thus arrives at the highest spiritual level as the "peak experience".

What is the "peak experience?" This is when a person experiences the peak of happiness. Consequently, it is not when a person attains power or fame when they are truly happy, but when they embody the meaning of self through love, good deeds, and serving others that they find true happiness.

Implant success patterns in your brain Do you know the phrase, "GIGO"? It's the abbreviation for "Garbage In, Garbage Out," meaning that if you put garbage in, garbage will come out. Frankly, this is a matter-of-fact logic, but what if we applied this phrase in a different way?

GIGO: "Good In, Good Out!"

We are able to implant success patterns in our heads. We are able to learn "success habits" or "success rhythms". For example, an elementary school student who incessantly gets failing marks does so because he or she wasn't given enough assignments where they could succeed, so they were unable to learn the feeling of success. In other words, they were deprived of the chance to develop a feeling of accomplishment.

Therefore, it is important for teachers to let students experience achievement. The tasks that teachers give should meet the level of the student, and must be interesting enough to trigger their motivation. This small feeling of accomplishment will give a taste of success to the students, and will become a valuable force when they take on other tasks in the future.

Happiness Guide

Your brain is you, and your brain is your life. Your life and happiness rely on how you use your brain. Enjoy a feeling of achievement by starting with things that are likely to succeed. Achievement brings more achievement and success is built on top of success. Experience of small success will bring bigger success.

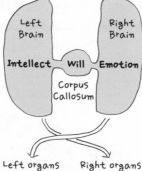

◀ I can do it

1. I will use reason(Left Brain) and imagination(Right Brain) to become happy. I will smile and think positively which will produce endorphins and make me feel happy.

2. I will memo my everyday thoughts and make sure not to miss any valuable ideas.

3. I will implant the patterns of success in my brain. I will learn "success habits" or "success rhythms". First, I will start with something fun, something I am confident in.

Reform Your Brain, Reform Your Fate

Zig Ziglar, a proponent of mind training, was walking down the stairs to a New York subway when he came across a hobo selling pencils. Ziglar gave the man a dollar and like other do-gooders declined the pencil, but then Ziglar went back, approached the man and said, "I'd like a pencil for the dollar I gave you earlier." As he received the pencil from the hobo, Ziglar said in a strong voice, "You are a businessman just like me. You are no longer a beggar."

The moment the hobo heard this, he thought, 'No, I'm not a beggar. I'm a businessman who sells pencils for a dollar each.' From that day forth, the man's image of self changed and his strength and courage was renewed. He repeated to himself, "I'm not a beggar. I'm a businessman. I'm a businessman. I'm a businessman who sells pencils," and with these words his fate and circumstances changed.

Later, this man became a successful businessman, and he went to Ziglar and told him, "What you said changed me. Because everyone else handed me a dollar and didn't bother to take my pencils, I always had an image of myself as a beggar. But you took a pencil and told me, 'You're a businessman just like me,' and this changed my life."

II

With All Your Strength: Intelligence Development

Power consists of physical power and psychological power.
Which is stronger? Of course it is the latter.
Intelligence Development is to strengthen the power to live
a challenging life.

4 *Blue Ocean in the Left Brain*

POWER OF PERCEPTION

A predisposition for intelligence   I was introduced to an Eastern medicine doctor a few days ago. An acquaintance was concerned for my health and brought the doctor to examine me since I tend to overexert myself with my work. I was touched by her considerate gesture and complied with her wishes. The doctor asked me a few questions, took my pulse and said, "You have a predisposition for intelligence."

He added that this was because I am a "solar person". Of course he advised me on other things as well. His diagnosis on my physical condition was quite accurate. But you're probably still wondering if there is such a thing as a "predisposition for intelligence".

Regardless whether the doctor's analysis was true or not, I am someone who must use my head for a living. Because I am the chief of a research institute, I am always on the lookout for information that will benefit the future. For me, information is an immense asset. I give many lectures and write many articles, but this doesn't mean I concentrate on the quantity of work I produce. I am always trying to produce qualitative ideas that have originality. Now you might think I'm being conceited, but these things about me are objective facts.

Due to the kind of work I do, people either ask me how high my IQ is or simply determine that I am smart. I don't deny their assertions, but I don't completely acknowledge that their assertions are correct either. I am not someone who idles away relying on my intelligence. I constantly try to find valuable new information. I read the latest trends when I look at billboards or store signs, absorb current fads through TV dramas and comedy programs, and I frequently find myself blown away by the amazing information I am able to glean from newspapers and magazines.

This kind of information is a great help in finding the hidden 'Blue Ocean' in the Left Brain. I can boldly say that I am one of the pioneers in this field.

Now why don't we take a journey into this hidden blue ocean?

The human body responds according to perception The Left Brain controls reason, in other words, thought. Thought produces emotion. And emotion is generally controlled by the Right Brain. Therefore, this means our Right Brain and Left Brain operate together. Let's look at the following example.

A man was sightseeing at Niagara Falls. He was so thirsty that he drank some of the water from the falls, but as he turned around he noticed a sign that said, "Poisson". He was so distressed at the thought that he had drunk poison that suddenly he felt intense abdominal pain as if his intestines were melting away. He had mistaken this word for the English word, "poison".

Other tourists saw how the man was suffering and quickly took him to the hospital. However, when the physician heard what had happened he only laughed at the man's story. The doctor told the bewildered patient, "Sir, what you saw on that sign wasn't the English word, 'poison,' but the French word 'poisson' that has another 's' in it. The word was 'fishing' or in other words the sign meant, 'Do not fish.'"

At the doctor's explanation, the stomach pains that the man

had been feeling disappeared and he went home a healthy man.

What does this story mean? It means that people feel the way they perceive.

Socrates was a person who could convert what most people would consider a misfortune into a blessing through optimism. He was a positive thinker who found opportunity for happiness in the worst conditions.

Xanthippe, was a loud woman who had a hot temper. People would ask him, "Why do you live with such a bad wife?"

He would answer, "Anyone who wants to be a master horseman rides the wildest horse. This is because when one gets used to dealing with an unruly horse, it is much easier to ride any other horse. If I'm able to endure this woman, there will be no one I won't be able to handle."

Another time, someone asked him how he tolerates his wife's ceaseless nagging, and Socrates answered, "Even the sound of a water mill becomes tolerable once you get used to the noise," and he laughed.

One day, his wife poured forth a barrage of complaints and

then threw a bucket of water on Socrates' head, but all Socrates said was: "A storm always follows thunder."

Any average person would have exploded with rage at Xanthippe's harsh words, but Socrates responded with wit and was able to control his emotions with his positive attitude. This is the power of perception. Within every emotion lies thought, hence we are able to control our emotions through optimistic thought.

LAW OF THOUGHT

Expect for the best and you will get the best: The Placebo Effect   Thought influences the body. One drastic example of this is 'the placebo effect,' which derived from the following event.

There was a pharmacist named Emile Cou in France. One day a woman came to him without a doctor's prescription and complained that she was so ill she thought she would die, but she couldn't go to the doctor's office because of the late hour. At first, Cou refused to help her because she didn't have a prescription, but feeling pity toward the woman he

Placebo

gave her a sugar pill, which wouldn't have any actual effect for the pain.

A few days later, Cou ran into the woman on the street, and to his surprise she said, "The pill was remarkable. I took one pill and I was cured. Thank you so much."

How could this be? The answer is this:

The patient trusted the pharmacist, and she believed in the pill that the pharmacist had given her. She was sure that she would get better, and this faith allowed her to be cured, regardless of the content of the pill.

At times, we forecast bad things for ourselves. This is

called 'nocebo effect,' the opposite to 'the placebo effect'. The problem is nocebo effect has much greater powers than the placebo effect. Thus, it is very important for us to think positively. When we choose to think in an optimistic way, our lives will flow with peace and happiness even when the worst hardships come our way.

Have high hopes and you will receive: The Pigmalion Effect

Something similar to 'the placebo effect' is 'the pigmalion effect'. This theory also shows the significance in the effects that come from having expectations.

Psychologist, Robert Rosenthal, proved this through research conducted on a group of grade school children. First, Rosenthal provided the teachers with IQ scores of the students in order to cause expectations from the teachers toward the children. Rosenthal hypothesized that the teachers would have higher hopes for the students with high IQ scores and encourage them or show other subtle differences toward them.

At the end of the semester Rosenthal's hypothesis proved to be correct. In short, the students who had high IQ's and received higher expectation from the teachers showed greater increase in school test scores than the other children. Also, results showed that children in lower grades were influenced more.

This is a good example of how significantly our minds affect our behavior. To the students with higher IQ's the teachers smiled more often, looked their way more, and showed more favorable reactions to their comments in class. Therefore, the students who received such higher expectations enjoyed going to school. Even if they happened to make a mistake, the teacher would offer tender words of encouragement, which allowed them to work harder on their school work. Consequently, it was proven that the expectations from the teachers displayed a much greater influence on the students than their initial IQ scores.

In this way, our thoughts have enormous effect not only in changing ourselves, but changing others as well.

OPEN THE WINDOW TO YOUR MIND

Break your preconceptions   Out in the middle of the ocean, a ship hit a rock and sunk. Nine of the crew survived the harsh ordeal and they arrived at an abandoned island. However, they were met with the worst environment imaginable. There was nothing to eat or drink.

Their only hope was for God to give them rain, or for a passing ship to come rescue them.

Eventually, only one member of the crew was left. He couldn't bear his burning thirst any longer and barely managed to get himself into the ocean, where he frantically drank the sea water. He couldn't taste any brininess or bitterness. In fact, the water was so sweet that his thirst was quenched in an instant. He walked up to the shore where he quietly lied down to await his death.

He woke up after a long sleep. The sailor was amazed to find that he was still alive. He thought it was strange, but there was no other way than to live off the sea water every day. Finally, a ship miraculously came by. The sea water was later analyzed, and it was discovered that fresh water constantly flowed from underground in that area. It turned out to be spring water fit to drink.

Preconceptions don't solve anything. The answer can be found only when those preconceived notions are broken.

Everybody has problems. On this, Karl Popper made the following definition on life: "Everything in life is basically problem solving."

I'd like to add something to this: "There is no problem in this world that can't be solved."

preconceptions

Ask a different question   This is a true incident that occurred at a condiment company.

Sales were declining with each day at this company, so they held an emergency meeting to come up with a counter-plan.

"How can we raise sales?"

The employees got together and came up with several ideas, but the low sales rate did not budge. Just then, one of the employees presented an innovative proposal.

"What if we made the holes in the condiment containers twice the size they are now?"

This ingenious idea was put to the test immediately and as a result sales doubled. The employee had asked a different question from the other workers. She didn't ask, "How will I raise sales?" Instead she had asked, "How will I make people buy condiments more often?"

The secret to bringing a change to your life is by asking a different question.(Kotaro Hisui, MottoTherapy; Finding Happiness in 3Seconds)

Using the Blue Ocean of the Left Brain

The Left Brain is a vast ocean of cogitation. In this ocean is a territory where no one has ever cast a net into. This territory, the 'Blue Ocean' is a territory of new possibilities. Let's utilize this 'Blue Ocean' to live a life where everything goes well. In order to do this, I offer you these two Blessings of the Rainbow.

－Think positively.
－Scatter the seed of wisdom.

I will further discuss these two principles in Chapter 5 and Chapter 6.

Happiness Guide

The Left Brain manages reason. Reason influences your emotions and body and leads you to action. Also, the information accumulated in the Left Brain is your strength and ultimately controls your health. In order to use the infinite 'blue ocean' hidden in your Left Brain, you have to be able to change your conceptions in various ways.

📢 I can do it

1. I will always look on the bright side. This way, I will achieve the best results.
2. I will accept new information without hesitation. I will see a larger world.
3. I will break any stereotypes that I have. I will feel new and fresh.

If Someone Complains about a Slow Elevator

Imagine that you are the owner of an office building. How will you respond if people complain that the elevator is too slow?

There are many ways to solve this problem. For example, you can add a new elevator, get work done to make a larger elevator, or you can get new tenants for your building and make sure their opening and closing hours don't overlap so that there isn't a rush for the elevator. There are many ways to solve this problem, but all the solutions mentioned above cost a lot of time and money.

What if you have to solve the problem with only a spare amount of time and money?

One office building landlord did just this.

"The elevator is so slow it's slowing down our work. We're going to vacate the building soon if this problem continues," tenants complained.

It was truly a difficult situation, but those complaints disappeared just the next day. The only thing that changed was this: a mirror had been installed on the wall of each floor next to the elevator.

It will cost a lot of money if you think in terms of 'how will I increase the number of elevators?' but this landlord had thought, 'How will I make it less irritating for people to wait for an elevator?'

If the question changes, so does the answer.

(Kotaro Hisui, MottoTherapy; Finding Happiness in 3Seconds)

5 *Blessing of the Rainbow 1 |*
Think Positively

OVERCOMING NEGATIVE THINKING

Everyone has a different way of thinking   I have
the privilege of meeting many people, which naturally causes
me to engage in conversations with diverse individuals with
various jobs and backgrounds. Because of this, I have realized that each individual has their own way of thinking.

Each person has their own line of thinking. For some people that line is very straight, so they accept what another person has to say quite literally. On the other hand, for some people that line bends to the left, which in turn makes them look
at another person through a refracting lens. At other times,
people's line of thinking curves to the right, where they ele-

vate the other person and expand on the other's comments.

Furthermore, one's way of thinking can generally be categorized according to type of occupation. I'm not saying this rule applies to everybody, but usually people in the military, teachers, and civil servants have solid principles and this reflects when they interact with other people. Someone who is an entrepreneur or head of a company generally is ready to take risks and has good problem solving skills.

Of course, each individual is different. They might be the complete opposite from their "category". The crux is each person has a thinking pattern they display out of habit. A person with a negative thinking system will only see the hazards even when a sure chance comes their way, but a person with a positive thinking pattern will find an opportunity in the worst conditions.

My conclusion is simple. A person's happiness and success is already determined according to the way that person tends to think. If you want a change in your life, first change the way you think. In order to make a path through a patch of weeds, one must first clear that path and tread on it repeatedly.

How and in what direction must we create our way of thinking?

During WWII, a woman named Thelma Thompson went to live in the Mojave Desert with her husband, who was deployed to a military training base. Everyday, Thelma was left all alone in their bungalow while her husband went off to work. Temperatures would rise to 115 degrees, and her food would be grainy with sand that blew from the harsh desert winds. There was no one around but the natives who did not speak English. She was devastated, and she expressed her bleak world to her father in a letter saying, "I can't live like this. Prison would be better than this."

However, her father sent a reply to her that contained just two lines.

"Two people look out the prison bars.

One person sees a muddy road, the other sees the stars."

Thelma Thompson was jolted by her father's letter, and those two lines changed her life. She went out and made friends with her neighbors, and studied the vast wilderness that was all around her. She later wrote a book on her studies called, Bright Ramparts. By changing her way of thinking she was able to transform from a prisoner of misery to a best selling author.

Are you going to look at the muddy road and live in despair, or are you going to look up at the stars and see hope? This is simply a matter of choice.

We must be able to look at the ordinary and see the valuable, even though it might not be apparent to the naked eye. Finding happiness and success is like having a keen eye and being able to find a pearl in the mud.

Hines Ward, voted MVP of Super Bowl XL, liked Mickey Mouse ever since he was a child. He even has a tattoo of Mickey holding a football on his left arm.

When Hines was a boy, he was teased and ostracized for having racially mixed heritage. His mother was Korean and father African American, but Hines was accepted by neither ethnic group. His father left early on and so his mother had to raise him alone in a land that was foreign to her, which caused much hardship and financial difficulty. However, whenever Hines was feeling low, Mickey Mouse was a friend

that would make him laugh.

Hines Ward made it his disposition to laugh. He laughs when he gets a bloody nose or an injury by an opponent during a game, he laughs when he drops the ball, and he laughs when he makes a touchdown. His laugh has made the Hines Ward who he is today.

This man's life offers us a lesson. With a positive self-image and optimistic way of thinking anyone can become a winner in life.

See the blessing beyond the affliction   There was an artist around the time of the Cultural Revolution in China who was accomplished at drawing horses. However, during the Cultural Revolution, he was prohibited from drawing, and so he became a vagrant and went from one place to another, cleaning stables. At first, he was full of anger and resentment and he showed his anger while he worked, but little by little he grew attached to the horses and he worked happily.

Finally after ten years, the Cultural Revolution came to an end, and before he knew it the artist had spent seven of those years working with horses. The artist took up his brush once again, and surprisingly his pictures flowed with vivacity more than ever before, even though he had not drawn a single picture during the past seven years. What was his secret?

Though the artist could not draw his horse paintings during the Cultural Revolution, he had spent all his time close to real horses. He was able to see the horses' physiology up front. Before, he'd only known the horse through theory and drawings, but after being near horses, he was able to paint a much more expert portrayal of the animal.

This is a story about the Cape of Good Hope.

For a long time, people called what was then thought to be the southern most tip of Africa, the Cape of Storms. The waters were so ferocious no one was able to get near the cape. However, in the 15th century, Portuguese explorer Vasco da Gama made an attempt and he passed through with success. Afterwards, the "Cape of Storms" was renamed the "Cape of Good Hope" by John II of Portugal. When Vasco da Gama passed through the rough seas, he came upon the world's most tranquil waters the Indian Ocean and the most beautiful shores.

The "Cape of Storms" had become the "Cape of Good Hope" in people's eyes after overcoming the wall of fear. The same rings true whenever we are faced with suffering or affliction.

Overcoming Passivity

In times of fear   During WWII 300 thousand U.S. soldiers lost their lives. But over one million U.S. civilians, who had sent their husbands and sons to war, had died from heart disease caused by anxiety, fear, and apprehension. Far more people died from anxiety and terror than from bullets.

According to a survey, of the things that cause people to worry and feel anxious about, 40% are things of the past, 50% are things of the future, and only 10% are about the present. This means over half of the world's population lives in anxiety about the future, which hasn't even occurred yet. There are so many cases where people die from heart illness because their nerves keep them awake at night.

US President Abraham Lincoln was able to endure with faith and prayer whenever he was overwhelmed by uneasiness. A Bible that he frequently read is kept in Washington D.C., and its pages are marked with his fingerprints. There is a part of the Book where his fingers left a deeper impression than the others.

"I prayed to the Lord, and he answered me; he freed me from all my fears."(Psalm 34:4)

Lincoln lived with the conviction that God will answer his prayers through every peril, such as the Civil War, and he will be saved from fear. He was able to make the great accomplishment of abolishing slavery by reading over and over this psalm until the pages became worn from his fingering.

Discard the image of the locust   In the Bible is the story of when the people of Israel fled from Egypt to go to God's Promised Land. When they had almost arrived at the land of Canaan, God told Moses to send a reconnaissance party to the new land.

However, the party came back in 40 days and reported different views. Ten out of the twelve men said this:

"And we saw giants there, the descendants of Anak. We felt as small as grasshoppers, and that is how we must have looked to them."(Numbers 13:33)

These people had felt they were as little as locusts compared to the giant race.

On the other hand, the remaining two, who were Jehovah and Caleb, told a completely different account.

"If the Lord is pleased with us, he will take us there and give us that rich and fertile land. Do not rebel against the

Lord and don't be afraid of the people who live there. We will conquer them easily. The Lord is with us and has defeated the gods who protected them; so don't be afraid." (Numbers 14:8-9)

How contrasting these reports are! Compared to the ones who compared themselves to locusts, these two thought of the enemy as their prey, giving themselves dignity and confidence. What was the basis for such confidence? It was the faith that they are the children of God and that "the Lord is with us."

The self-image of locusts and the self-image of unconquerable children of God! Which image of self do you live with?

Thought produces emotion. Thought also brings change to your actions. Finally, thought changes your life. Therefore, the wise advise this:

"Be careful how you think; your life is shaped by your thoughts."(Proverbs 4:23)

CHALLENGE YOURSELF

Two different faxes   Two salesmen, who worked for a shoe manufacturing company, went to Africa on a business trip. They went to observe the potential of Africa as a new marketing frontier. However, when they arrived in Africa they were stunned by the circumstances which they were met by. The people there didn't wear shoes! They went around barefoot. After surveying the region for a while the two salesmen each sent a fax to the company headquarters.

One of them sent a telex that said, "Impossible to export shoes. Potential 0%. Everyone barefoot."

And the other salesman sent a fax that said, "Goldmine. Potential 100%. Everyone barefoot."

According to this point of view, the person with a negative outlook saw 0% potential whereas the person with an optimistic view saw 100% potential in the situation. This is not a discrepancy. No one is right or wrong. They both see truth according to each perspective. Now, how do you want to look at things?

I can do it   I saw a very touching story on TV a few years ago. It was the life story of Tae-yun Kim, head of the TYK Group, which consists of Lighthouse Worldwide Solutions, Morningplanet, Datastore X, Angelhealing along with many other feats. Her motto has become her trademark:

"He can do it. She can do it. Why not me?"

Tae-yun Kim never had the chance to spread her wings when she was growing up in her small hometown. Then, at the age of 23, she followed her family and immigrated to the US. Even in the US, she was discriminated against because of her race. When she was running a Taekwondo gym from what she had learned in her childhood, and when she was running her own business, she had numerous trials to overcome. Nonetheless, she braced herself and thought, 'He can do it. She can do it. Why not me?'

Finally, she made her achievement. Lighthouse, which Kim currently runs, is a blue chip company, making a yearly 150,000,000,000 won(approximately 1.5 million dollars). And she has spread her ventures to environmental endeavors, computers, Internet, and cosmetics. Not only that, she is the grand master of the Taekwondo gym, Jung SuWon Martial Art Wellness Center, and is host of her own Tae-yun Kim Show, standing amongst the most prominent American figures today.

This is what she says:

"You should never forget that a person's attitude plays a significant role in determining their life. Tormenting yourself and being anxious that something won't work is simply a shortcut to a person's ruin. That kind of mentality is the biggest enemy to your growth. Why think you can't do something that everyone else can? Everything starts at the point when you have the confidence that you can do anything. Have hope in your heart and believe that you can achieve and this will be the beginning to your success. 'He can do it. She can do it. Why not me?'

Happiness Guide

Happiness and success depend on how you think. You will be owner of your life if you throw away your negative and passive thoughts and change them to positive and active thoughts. The future is yours when you challenge yourself with the faith that "I can do it."

◄€ I can do it

1. I will make a change by repaving my path with positive and active thoughts.
2. I will not be afraid of something that hasn't happened yet. Worry and anxiety block progressive thinking.
3. I will challenge myself endlessly. If someone else can do it, so can I.

◀▶ *It's Still You*

Do you remember Superman? The hero who played superman, Christopher Reeve?

One day this hero fell from his horse and was paralyzed. This caused him so much agony that he thought, 'I'd rather die.'

When his mother came into his hospital room, he told her that he'd rather be taken off the respirator and die than retain his life like this.

Afterwards, his wife, Dana, arrived at the hospital. Reeve told the same thing to his wife, and his wife said something remarkable:

"It's still you."

She took her hands and touched her husband's cheeks, her husband who was paralyzed and couldn't even breathe on his own and she said, "As long as your brain is alive, you're still the same person. Please just live for me."

These words from his wife, Dana, saved Superman. Henceforth, he became a symbol of hope and courage to people around the world. Until his death he spoke each year at the UN as a spokesman for the disabled. Among so many great speakers, he was the most inspirational because he had overcome the impossible and showed people that a future does exist.

What made the human Christopher Reeve into a great man? It was just like his wife told him. He still had a right to live. Like this, positive thinking will give you hope in any kind of situation.

6 *Blessing of the Rainbow 2* |
Scatter the Seed of Wisdom

FIND THE SPRING OF WISDOM

Hunter of wisdom   I pride myself in being a hunter of wisdom in life and having an expert eye for distinguishing it. I'm not being delusional. This is my attitude and expectation of life.

As the Blessing of the Rainbow became widely adored, I have received continual requests to write recommendation notes for new books. I don't accept all of the requests, but only choose the books which I think are truly good, and everytime I do this I like to directly and indirectly show myself as a "Hunter of wisdom".

I want to ask readers, from the bottom of my heart, to be

hunters of wisdom. A wise man once said, "Happy the man who meditates on wisdom, and reflects on knowledge; who ponders her ways in his heart, and understands her paths; who pursues her like a scout, and lies in wait at her entry way." (Ecclesiastes 14:20-22)

Let's each go in search of the spring of wisdom that will guide us through our lives.

The most important thing   We live in a time where we feel obligated to accumulate as much information as we can from the deluge of information that engulfs us. Here is a noteworthy story for us.

A scholar was crossing a river and he asked the boatman, "Do you know how to compose a poem?"

"No sir, I'm afraid I don't."

"Ah, then you haven't experienced the true taste of life. Hmm…I wonder if you would know the teachings of Confucius and Mencius?"

"No sir, I'm afraid I don't."

"Ah, then you don't know about human duty. Hmm… would you know how to read?"

"No, I'm afraid I'm a complete ignoramus."

"Oh my! Then why do you live?"

Just at that moment, the boat hit a rock and started to sink. This time, the boatman asked the scholar, "Sir, do you know how to swim?"

"No, I'm afraid I don't."

"Then you are as good as dead."

Perhaps we are like the scholar in this story. We boast of the vast amount of knowledge we own, but when it comes down to it, do we really know 'how to live'? There are many pleasures and worthy things in the world, but what happens when we suddenly hit a rock and can't save our own lives? What use are all those things?

Could it be possible that the boatman, though not quite so knowledgeable, is the wise one?

Find wisdom in information   People who changed history were people who knew the significance of lifelong study. The new millennium is the era of information revolution. Today, information is considered as vital as life itself. People are owners of information, and the owners who are sagacious enough to apply their information to the fullest extent are the ones who are sought after. It's not enough to simply have information; you must be able to create it as well. In other words, society seeks people who are able to generate knowledge.

Hoarding information is not the answer. The answer is to procure wisdom out of the piles of knowledge around you.

From a very early age, Bill Gates, founder of Microsoft, vividly showed how information can be an asset. He enjoyed reading ever since he was a little boy, only leaving his father's study to go to school, peering into one after another of his father's books. His favorite book when he was seven-years-old was the World Book Encyclopedia. There was no one his age who read such an immense volume of books.

It has been the same after he grew up too. He applies his fundamental rule for lifelong study when he goes on vacation, always choosing a theme for each trip. For example, when he went to Brazil several years back, the theme for the trip was "physics," and during the whole time he devoured books on physics. Not only that, in order to keep up with the quickly developing high technology of the times, he invites science experts and listens to detailed reports about technological advancement.

Bill Gates, he found wisdom among countless bits of information. Therefore, he didn't stop at being an international magnate, but became a philanthropist who amazes the world.

SCATTERING THE SEED

Immerse yourself   There is an old Chinese proverb, 'Read a book one-hundred times and the meaning will come to you naturally(讀書百遍意自見).' Korean scholars used this method to comprehend the profound teachings of the wise.

It is truly an excellent method of reading and a great discipline. If you read a sentence one-hundred times aloud, you are not only understanding the sentence with your head, but comprehending it with your whole mind and body. The words have already seeped into your body. In other words, studying was a way to cultivate one's character for Korean scholars.

Recite and it will come true   One of the beliefs among the Native Americans is that if a person repeats something over ten-thousand times then that something will undeniably come true. If you recite words of wisdom good things will happen.

It's a practice that is shared in customs all around the world.

French chemist and psycho therapist, Emile Cou used the effect of repetitive speech and instigated great development in the field of 'self-reform'. He simply instructed his patients to repeat daily, "Everyday in every way, I'm feeling better and better." This very simple method reaped amazing results on treatment of various illnesses.

Following this success, Dr. Johannes Schultz, who was doing research on accelerating the recovery of patients, was able to go one step farther. He first put his patients in a relaxed state, then he encouraged them to express optimistic messages out loud, as well as visualizing these messages. Through this technique the messages were immediately conveyed to the patients' subconscious and helped them immensely to recover their physical and mental health.

WISDOM THAT SHINES THROUGH DURING CRISIS

Overcoming obstacles   Going through hard times as an unknown writer, W. Somerset Maugham was just able to get his first novel published. However, the publishing company wasn't up for putting in a lot of money to promote a novel by an unknown writer.

After many days of struggling to come up with an original idea to get the awareness out to the public, Maugham finally made a break through. He immediately ran to the newspaper office and found the person in charge of the classified section. Maugham handed him this copy to run in the newspaper:

"Young millionaire, lover of sports, cultivated, with good taste of music and a patient and empathetic character wishes to marry any young and beautiful girl that resembles the heroine of W.S. Maugham's new novel."

Immediately after this ad appeared in the paper Maugham's book started flying off the shelves. Not a week had passed and already his books were out of stock in all book stores.

A great writer was able to become famous due to his quick wit and wisdom.

A wealthy jeweler discovered a rare and precious stone during a trip in Europe. He gave an incredible amount of money and bought the stone, all the while bubbling with excitement at the thought of taking the gem back home and selling it for a higher price. However, he later discovered a flaw in the stone that he hadn't detected at the time of purchase.

'Oh my, what shall I do about this flaw⋯.'

He didn't know what to do.

Appraisers all gave him the same response that the flaw decreases the value of the stone. Not only was he unable to sell at the purchased price, but the offers just kept getting lower. The jeweler spent much time mulling over his situation. 'How can I raise the value of the stone to its original price?'

After putting in a lot of thought he came up with a solution. He was going to carve a rose on the flaw.

What was the result? With the simple carving of the rose, the value of the gem increased several times its original cost. It became a piece of art that everyone wanted to own.

To bring out a flaw that you have been trying to hide and using it to your advantage, this is wisdom.

Mind control   One day King David summoned a lapidary and gave the following instructions.

"Make a ring for me. On the ring, engrave words to control myself when I get overly excited after winning a battle. Also, the passage must be able to save me when I fall into despair."

The craftsman soon created a beautiful ring, but he couldn't come up with a passage to suit the King's wishes. Finally, the craftsman went to Prince Solomon for help.

The prince suggested the phrase, "This too shall pass!" He explained that with these words the King's pride will subside at victory, and his face will brighten up when in despair.

A pithy saying that a person accidentally comes upon can determine that person's life.

Happiness Guide

The words of wisdom are the light which drives out the darkness within you. If you recite those words and engrave them in your mind, they will be the seed to overcoming obstacles and eliminating fear. They will change cons to pros, make you a better conversationalist, and govern your thoughts.

◀≡ I can do it

1. I will post a saying or Bible verse that I like where I can see it and I will recite it as frequently as possible.
2. When despair, fear, or depression overwhelms me, I will drive those feelings out with the light from the words of wisdom.
3. I will offer the words of wisdom to a neighbor in distress.

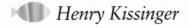 *Henry Kissinger*

Former U.S. Secretary of State, Henry Kissinger, was a man who moved the world as a politician and a diplomat. He was such a leading figure at the time that people went as far as to say 'Nixon was President, but Kissinger moved the world.'

Henry Kissinger was a Jew who had emigrated from Germany to the US. His English speech was never eloquent. In spite of this, the knowledge he had attained from reading the Bible as a boy governed him all through his life and played a key role in putting him on the stage of international politics. He said that every political principle is in the Bible.

With All Your Heart: Emotional Development

The heart is where our sensitivity lies.
There is a world of dreams in our hearts.
Emotional development is the key to a creative life.

7 Blue Ocean in the Right Brain

POTENTIAL OF THE RIGHT BRAIN

The way I read   I devour books. Recently, I haven't had the time to enjoy reading as much as I used to, but every so often when I drop by a book store I gain a heap of new information just by taking a look around. The part I concentrate on when encountering a book for the first time is the preface and table of contents. I also read the epilogue in great detail if there happens to be one. Once I've read these sections, I can roughly measure the outline of the book. Through my experience as a writer, I know that if the writing is as it should be, the essential idea of the book will be saturated into the introduction, table of contents, and epilogue.

When I read the main body of a book I scan the text in a diagonal line across the page and don't scrutinize all the words. I can judge in an instant whether the text on a page will offer any "new information" by connecting the words that catches my attention at first glance. By instinct I am able to detect where the key sentences are hidden, and when I spot one I zoom into that sentence and make sure to read it before going on. It isn't difficult to discern the meaning of the sentence or phrase because I link it to the key words that I've collected in my head so far. This whole process occurs in just a few seconds. Of course, this kind of reading manner has its pitfalls and limitations, but at the same time it is surprisingly efficient and scientific.

In neurophysiologic terms, this reading method is a technique that largely utilizes the Right Brain. The only part of the process which utilizes the Left Brain is when I "zoom-in," but the rest is a process that maximizes the Right Brain's association capacity.

Elevate your mood by using your Right Brain
Your mouth gets watery when you think of plums or apricots. Just thinking about ice cream makes you feel good. These phenomena occur because the Right Brain is in charge of our emotions.

The Right Brain can make you feel good or feel bad for no

apparent reason. Dopamine, the so-called "satisfaction hormone," is discharged when the Right Brain imagines something pleasant. Dopamine is a characteristic neurotransmitter that makes humans able to demonstrate higher levels of mental ability and creativity that is not apparent in other animals.

The human brain structure is designed so as not to cross-examine a person's present emotion. When a person is full of joy and pleasant feelings the memory system does not broach negative thoughts such as bills that have to be paid or whether or not one will lose one's job. This is called the "mood-congruity hypothesis". The gist of this theory is this: the human memory system has a tendency to recall events of a certain mood that coincide with the current mood a person is in.

In addition, the Right Brain is also concerned with instinct, creativity, and high levels of mental capacity.

The great men and women who live on throughout history are people who demonstrated the ability of their Right Brain.

Leonardo da Vinci was one of the most renowned geniuses. He had already envisioned the steamboat, helicopter, diving suit, elevator, automobile, excavator, parachute, telescope and much more 500 years ago. How was he able to think of these things with the same brain that everyone else has? The answer is 'his imagination'. He enjoyed imagining things and he was gifted in making his musings into reality.

Thomas Edison was deemed a dunce and was expelled from school just three months after he had started elementary school. He only received three months of school education, but he left tremendous achievements. He invented the light bulb and the phonograph and so many other devices that he holds a world record of 1,093 inventions.

What all of these great inventors and thinkers have in common is that their inspiration came from sparks of images more than from logical thinking. For them, reason was merely a means to convey their images to the rest of the world.

THE RIGHT BRAIN OPERATES AUTOMATICALLY

You are what you see and hear   It is not an exaggeration to declare that we are governed by the things we see and hear. Humans have evolved relying much on sight.

According to psychology education statistics, human learning is accomplished through 67% sight, 7% hearing, and 6% of taste/smell/touch. Also human memory consists of things we hear 10%, things we see 50%, making our memories comprised of things we see and hear a total of 80%.

Yulgok was a rare accomplished scholar and sage born in Korea and this was purely due to "seeing and hearing" his mother's teachings. Shinsaimdang, Yulgok's mother, represents the model mother figure for Koreans. Whenever she had a chance, she taught her children courtesy and she set an example by practicing good decorum herself.

Shinsaimdang herself was influenced from the things she saw and heard while she was being raised. She was the second child of five siblings who all grew up in her maternal grandparents' home in the town of Gangreung. She grew up grinding ink for her grandfather everyday and always had a brush in her hand, and so early on she developed an unusual talent for calligraphy and painting. As a result, her own seven children grew up watching her and they always had brush and ink close at hand. Today many calligraphy writings and paintings are left behind by her first child, a daughter, Maechang; Yulgok achieved success as a prominent scholar; and the seventh sibling, Woo(瑀), is also renowned as a calligrapher and painter. These accomplishments that highlight Korean cultural history did not occur simply by coincidence.(Young Ahn, Everlasting Moonbeam, Shinsaimdang)

Like this story, what we see and hear is beyond perceiving things as is. The things we come across become deeply rooted in our subconscious and affect us constantly. Therefore, what we see, and the operations of the Right Brain on the images we see are extremely important.

The subconscious determines success or failure

Here is an interesting experiment which was conducted on a group of elementary students in the U.S.

The teacher who partook in the experiment told her students: "According to a recent study, children with blue eyes have a higher learning aptitude than children with brown eyes."

After telling her students this bit of uncertified information, she had the children write the color of their eyes on a card and hang them around their necks. The children were monitored for a week and the results were as follows.

Learning motivation for children with brown eyes dropped, and the blue-eyed children became drastically better in class. Then, the teacher told the students, "There have been reports that the experimental results were wrong. In fact, brown-eyed children do better in class than blue-eyed children."

What were the results? As you can guess, this time the children with brown eyes excelled in class and learning ambition for the children with blue eyes dropped.

Accordingly, a person can change according to their self-image.

The images sculpted in your subconscious will operate as limitations on yourself. If you don't change those images it will be impossible for you to leap toward a better future.

The power of the left brain manifests itself clearly in the sports world as well. An athlete who is unable to put the abilities of the Left Brain to good use will not be victor no matter how talented that person is. You will flourish much more when you try to improve yourself and bring out your own potential, not when you try to triumph over someone else.

Great athletes say, "If you want to set a world record, first you have to make yourself the best."

JUST AS YOU PICTURED IT

Image training   The images inside the head of an outstanding athlete definitely were not molded in a day. Those images need to be trained, just like physical training.

The University of Illinois conducted a fascinating experiment with the university's basketball team. The team was divided into three groups; A, B, C, and the players in group A practiced shooting hoops for a month, the players in group B didn't have any shooting practice for a month, and group C imagined shooting, scoring and getting better and better at their skill for 30 minutes every day, i.e. they only had image training.

One month passed and results were astounding. First, as anyone would expect, group B, which didn't train at all didn't make any progress. However, both group A, which practiced shooting everyday in the gym, and group C, which trained mentally through visualization, saw the same amount of progress with of 25% increase in field goal percentage.

This experiment shows how effective seeing with your mind, that is having 'vision,' can be.

When you draw an image in your head, it has the same impact as it would physically. The human brain cannot easily distinguish between what happens for real and what we make up. In other words, in a situation where there is nothing, but the brain feels something as if it exists, then that thing truly exists for that person. Therefore, the sharper the image, the more probable it is for that image to become reality.

The deeper you etch the image of accomplishment in your mind, the better the chances for you to make that accomplishment in life. If you have negative images such as, 'I'm no good in school,' or 'I can't do that,' then you will have negative results. However, if you visualize yourself doing well in an exam or winning a prize, then these things will be reinforced in your Right Brain and you will have better chances of succeeding.

Use the Blue Ocean in the Right Brain

The Right Brain is a vast ocean of imagination. This is a 'Blue Ocean,' where no one has yet pitched a net into it is a territory of endless possibilities. Use this blue ocean to create a life where everything goes well with the next two Blessings of the Rainbow.

— Nurture a dream.
— Believe in achieving.

I will further discuss these two principles in Chapter 8 and 9.

Happiness Guide

The Right Brain manages emotion and is a treasury of imagination. While the Left Brain operates by passing through the circuit of reason, the Right Brain operates immediately by the influence of images which are engraved in your subconscious. Therefore, the way to raise the potential of your Right Brain to its fullest extent is through image training.

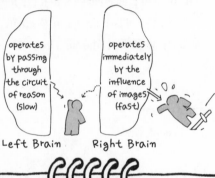

operates by passing through the circuit of reason (slow)

operates immediately by the influence of images (fast)

Left Brain   Right Brain

I can do it

1. I will try to use the imagination and creativity of my Right Brain to my greatest extent. Through this I will improve any inconveniences around me and create something new.

2. I will maintain good feelings within me and live a happy life using the imaginative power of my Right Brain. In other words, I will think of good people, beautiful scenery, touching memories, and heighten my present happiness.

3. I will start with image training before I begin something. I will imagine myself doing the job perfectly and will act accordingly.

Mock Training

Do you remember the words of Neil Armstrong when he first landed on the Moon? The first step he took on the Moon's surface he said these great words:

"That's one small step for man, one giant leap for mankind."

However, in the communication records of NASA there is something else that he said after this, which no one remembers. He said, "It was just like a drill. It was just like we planned it."

What this means is that before he went into outer space he'd had thorough practice on Earth of every possibility that might occur in space. His training helped him when he landed on the Moon. Therefore, the function of our Right Brain will develop if we do mock training with our minds beforehand and it will be a strong foundation for us to succeed in difficult situations.

Practice like it's the real thing. Draw an image in your mind of releasing your anxiety. You will never find yourself get perplexed when the real situation occurs. If you experience success in your head, you are sure to succeed in real life. Not to mention, you will become fearless and you will come to enjoy imagining critical situations.

Try drawing images of your day's schedule as you wake up in the morning. Developing this as your routine will make you a true victor in the intense competitive world.

8 *Blessing of the Rainbow 3* |
Nurture a dream

DREAMS COME TRUE

A gift for my nephew   My family was financially
troubled while I was growing up.

My father had come to Seoul from the North with nothing
but the shirt on his back. He educated himself and made his way
through college. When he graduated, he became a reporter for
the Hapdong News Agency and aspired for greatness. However,
soon thereafter the Korean War broke out, but my father didn't
make it out of Seoul and he was captured by the Communists.
He was forced against his will to commit "treachery". It was a
traitorous act since ultimately he was helping out the
Communists. Thus, when Seoul was reclaimed by the Allies on

September 28, 1950, my father was ferreted out along with the other traitors and after a summary trial they were executed by a firing squad. However, my father was saved with the help of an officer from the South Korean Army, under one condition; he had to enlist in the South Korean Army immediately.

He finished his term in the South Korean military and went south to live in my mother's hometown of Seoshin, a town located in the southern bay of Kyeonggi Province(approximately 2 hr drive from Seoul), where he became a government employee at the township office. Subsequently, he became tormented by the guilt of committing treachery. On top of that, he was agonized at being separated from the rest of his family who was in the North. He began to drink heavily and paid no attention to financial matters.

My family moved to Seoul when I was in the fourth grade to a neighborhood called Nangok, which had become a refugee community. That was when my family first started dealing briquette and rice from our home. We delivered rice and briquette, which was a main source of heating at the time, and this income helped sustain our household.

Time passed, but we were under no circumstance to be burdened by tuition fees, so I entered Yuhan Technical High School under a full scholarship. Though I was in a school that teaches technical skills, I still wanted to go to college. Once a teacher caught me studying English during shop and he smacked me across my face several times, fast and hard.

I endured and eventually when I was accepted at Seoul National University in the College of Engineering, my homeroom teacher thought highly of me and offered words of encouragement, "I have no doubt that you will become a great scholar."

However, I continued to be plagued by the course I had taken even after I entered the university I had so hoped to attend. I adapted well to my studies, but I was sure I had a higher aptitude for a career which dealt with people rather than with machines. I decided I wanted to become a doctor or a lawyer, but it was already too late. I was busy trying to eke out a living, and so I had faced the question too late; "What do I want to become?"

I went on to the next grade, but it was time for me to enlist in the military. Soon after I got commissioned in the Navy OCS(Officer Candidate School), my nephew was born. At the news of my nephew's birth, I wrote a poem for him to read later on. I put the poem in a picture frame and sent it home. This is what I wrote:

Little boy,
What do you see so far away
through your eyes that hold the black night,

sparkling like jewels.

Does your heart flutter at those dreams,

dreams of finding a single kindling of truth?

Your dreams shall be a bridge

between this rugged world and your visions

set on the white clouds floating by far up in the sky.

How good it feels to shout across the open plains,

But earnestly, your dreams will be the silent touchstone

of history.

Like the seas which are opened from the rivers,

the rivers opened from the streams,

people find their source from meaning.

Hope with high spirits is the only way

we can live.

Surprising study results by Harvard　　　There is a famous study which was conducted by Harvard University on the influence of a person's goal, i.e. a person's dream, on one's life. The people chosen for the study all had similar IQ's, educational levels, and grew up in similar backgrounds. The results were astounding.

Of the participants, 27% said they didn't have a goal, 60% had vague goals, 10% said they have relatively short-term goals, and only 3% said they have specific long-term goals.

After researching these participants for 25 years an interesting conclusion came about.

The 3% who said they have specific long-term goals had become important figures in all sorts of social fields after the twenty-five years. Of those 3% are self-made men, and most have become influential leading figures in society.

The 10% who said they have short-term goals maintained a social status of upper-middle class. By achieving their goals in several short courses they were able to construct a stable basis for their lives and became professionals, indispensible to society. For example, there are doctors, lawyers, architects, and entrepreneurs in this group.

The 60% who had vague goals remained in the lower-middle class. They all led stable lives, but they hadn't shown the remarkable success that the 10% had.

The 27% who didn't have any goals is the group we must pay attention to. They were living in the lowest conditions, showed repeated cycles of employment and unemployment, and only waited for society to relieve them from their situation. They resented others and society.

Which group do you belong to? The 3%, 10%, or 60%? Your answer determines your future. This is a grim standard. You must make a decision now to belong among the 3% or at least the 10%.

The Law of Seeing   How can a dream(= goal) become reality by holding onto it for a long time? The 'Law of Seeing' from the Bible explains this.

The first example is Abraham. God promised Abraham many offspring and plenty of land, and He had Abraham look toward this promise until it came true. He showed Abraham a myriad of stars and countless grains of sand and gave him the dream of having as many children as those stars and grains of sand.

"Look at the sky and try to count the stars; you will have as many descendants as that."(Genesis 15:5)

When God gave Abraham his land he first showed the land of Canaan and the north, south, east, west, and then kept His promise to give him that land. In short, God used the 'power of seeing' on Abraham. Because Abraham looked to the promised blessings from God through his firm faith in Him, Abraham was able to later earn those blessings.

What about the story of Jacob? He stayed at his father-in-law Laban's house for 20 years, serving him faithfully until one day Jacob implored that Laban let Jacob leave for his homeland. Laban asked what Jacob would like for his wages, but Jacob said he wouldn't take anything from Laban. Instead he made a deal with Laban, saying he would pasture and keep Laban's flock and all he wanted were the speckled and spot-

ted sheep, the black lambs, and the spotted and speckled goats from Laban's herd. Laban agreed, but of course he removed all the speckled and spotted animals from the flock and hid them first. Nonetheless, while praying, Jacob had received a vision from God to use this 'law of seeing'. Thus, Jacob used visual impressions on the flock by peeling rods of poplar, almond, and plane trees so that they had white stripes. "He placed these branches in front of the flocks at their drinking troughs. He put them there, because the animals mated when they came to drink."(Genesis 30:38)

Moreover, Jacob didn't show the striped rods to just any sheep. "When the healthy animals were mating, Jacob put the branches in front of them at the drinking troughs, so that they would breed among the branches."(Genesis 30:41)

Finally, Jacob's 'law of seeing' paid off. The weak became Laban's and Jacob got the strong. "In this way Jacob became very wealthy. He had many flocks, slaves, camels, and donkeys."(Genesis 30:43)

We should learn from Abraham and Jacob. Persistently look toward a dream and nurture that dream, and when it is time, that dream is sure to come true.

WHAT KIND OF DREAM WILL YOU DREAM?

Be ambitious   'Boys, be ambitious!'

This adage always appeared in English text books when I was in middle school. The older I get, the more I agree with these words. Naturally, 'ambition' should be regarded in a constructive aspect. The size of your dream as a child determines the size of your life.

The word, 'limit' is simply a meek excuse for failure. Limits always make people rely too much on 'experience'. It kills your determination, constantly chasing you around like a foreboding shadow.

Many people underestimate themselves and lower their goals, going along with the "smaller" successes in their lives. Big ambition brings forth big success. If you don't have ambition, you will not be able to achieve your goals.

There is a fish called, 'Koi,' that is commonly raised in Japanese households. This carp will only grow to about 2-3 inches when kept in a small tank, but when kept in a large aquarium or a pond it grows to a length of 6-10 inches, and when it lives freely in a river it grows up to 35-50 inches. Koi can become stunted fish or majestic carp according to the size of the world they live in. Our thoughts are like the environment which Koi are put into; we will grow if we think bigger and dream bigger. There is no limit to the size of our minds.

Find a role model among famous heroes

One needs to be in the presence of greatness in order to become a great person. What this means is people are raised to be what they are, and it also means that they need role models.

However, it's not easy to meet a great man in person to be your role model. At times like these, there are books, especially the classics, where there are plenty of role models to take after.

The University of Chicago is nicknamed the "Nobel Prize Kingdom". This is due to the fact that 79 of their alumni, researchers, and professors have become Nobel Laureates. In its early years, the University of Chicago lost all its potential students to Ivy League schools in the east since it had comparatively a much shorter history. In spite of its rough start, the reason that this university was able to become a "Nobel Prize Kingdom" was chiefly due to the hard work of Robert

M. Hutchins, the originator of Educational Perennialism.

When Dr. Robert Hutchins became president of the University of Chicago, he established an undergraduate curriculum where the students had to read 100 select books. By reading those books, he basically had the students discover common truths which are constant throughout all ages, and presented them with role models that the students could look to for guidance in their search for truth. In other words, he was telling them to meet great people in the classics and become great people themselves. This kind of education was how so many people from the University of Chicago could become Nobel Laureates.

Nurture dreams that are just   When I was a youth, I had a friend whom I had a common goal with. This friend's dream was to go out into society and earn a lot of money, and my dream was to do a lot of good things for society. We made a pact. After this friend earned a lot of money, I would use his money for a good cause.

Later, we lost touch and twenty years had gone by. One day, with a touch of luck I got back in touch with that friend and we met. He told me he had been searching for me all this time. He had become president of a rising medium-sized enterprise. He remembered the promise we had made back in our days of youth and donated a large sum of money for me to use. We bought a piece of land with the money and our current research center was built there.

Actually, he had gone through rough times. He later told me that he had failed in a number of businesses, but he held onto his dream. He was going to be rich and use his money for good causes no matter what. Needless to say, the vow he had made with me years ago had played a part in his determination.

Even now he has a dream. He wants to be a person who can offer even more help. The reason he was able to realize his dream was because his dream was just.

In Order To Make A Dream Come True

Utilize the "laws"   Brian Tracy, a famous success theorist in the US, claims that just like there are natural laws, there are also mental laws. According to him, it is when your thoughts and actions correspond to these mental laws that your life will run smoothly. If a problem should arise there is no doubt that this is because you have broken the "law".

The following are a few laws that will help you accomplish your dream.

First is the "Law of Belief". This means that whatever you believe, with feeling, it will be realized. For instance, if you believe you will absolutely achieve your goal, you will be able to progress toward your goal regardless what may cross your path. However, if you believe that accomplishment is determined by fate or coincidence, you will easily get discouraged when something doesn't go as planned. Needless to say, it is the optimist who designs and creates their future. And they will succeed at all costs.

The second law is the "Law of Attraction". It means that people are living magnets. In other words, we attract the things that agree with our thoughts into our lives. Happy people pull in happy people, people who think about financial riches attract ideas and chances to earn lots of money. Like this, if you concentrate on what you truly want, the law of attraction is bound to start working.

The third is the "Law of Correspondence," and this means that your inner world is reflected onto your outer world. Everything in life moves from the inside-out. Therefore, you yourself must first change. When you fill your internal state with dreams and hope, this will emanate to your outer world and your life will change accordingly.

Goethe once said, "One must be something to be able to do something."

Believe that your dream will come true(The Law of Belief), and attract what you want(The Law of Attraction), and work to harmonize your inner self with it(The Law of Correspondence) in order to make your dream a reality.

Visualize   The best method to realizing your dream is visualization. Set an ideal and successful vision of yourself and think of this everyday. You can make it come true.

Brian Tracy says there are 4 elements in the visualization process. Let's see how it works with goal achievement.

The first element is frequency. The number of times you visualize your goal and future behavior has a powerful impact on your thoughts, feelings, and actions. The frequency of visualization reflects how much you really want something, and this operates to intensify your desire and belief that you will achieve.

The second element is vividness. You must imagine your dream with clarity and specificity. Successful people are able to give a clear account of what they want. However, people who are unsuccessful are obscure and uncertain.

The third element is intensity. This refers to the amount of emotion you put into visualizing your dream. If we want something, we get excited about it, get absorbed in it and passionate about it. If you intensely believe that you will achieve your goal, this will accelerate the realization of it.

The last element of visualization is duration. This refers to the amount of time you keep your dream in your mind. The longer you imagine, the more often you visualize, the higher the potential that your dream will actually be achieved. If you do this, your visualizations will become commands into your subconscious and your mind will control you to make yourself in keeping with those views.

Let's draw ideal pictures in our minds whenever we get a chance. Through this, our subconscious will control the way we talk, act, and feel so that we fit into the image of success we have created, and we will move toward achieving our dreams.

Enjoy the process   If you want to realize your dreams you must enjoy the process. If you simply become goal oriented and begin thinking of the process as a tedious duty, you're liable to give up mid-way.

In a famous speech delivered by Albert E. N. Gray, known to us as, 'The Common Denominator of Success,' Gray stated that the successful people he had observed had the following in common.

"Successful men are influenced by the desire for pleasing results. Failures are influenced by the desire for pleasing methods and are inclined to be satisfied with such results as can be obtained by doing things they like to do. The common denominator of success the secret of every man who has ever been successful lies in the fact that he formed the habit of doing things that failures don't like to do."

Albert Gray is right. If you want to make your dream come true, you have to make 'what you have to do' into 'what you want to do.'

Gus Hiddink, Korea's 2002 World Cup soccer coach and hero, first met the Korean national team and told them this: "Enjoy soccer." Hiddink always emphasized that the Korean team cannot make it to the second round with only patriotism.

These days Korean soccer is much better, but whenever I watch it I feel like I'm watching a taekwondo match. The fighting spirit is strong, but they lack flexibility. On the other hand, how about Brazilian soccer? They are indescribably lithe. Anyone would agree that it's a work of art. Their body movements derive from the enjoyment of soccer. Why did people around the world go mad over Zidane, member of the Art Soccer club as well as former French national team star? It was not only because of his agile movements, but also because of his superb timing. These qualities cannot be attained from aggressive practicing alone.

Truly enjoy yourself. Then you will be a pro. Passionately enjoy yourself. Then you will be a matchless star. The student who finds pleasure in studying and learning is the one who excels. The professor who enjoys teaching delivers the best lectures. The businessman who has fun doing business becomes rich.

Happiness Guide

Everyone dreams. However there's a difference in nurturing a dream and simply having a dream. The key is to persist in nourishing that dream. Anyone who has made a great accomplishment in history was someone who nurtured their dream with tenacity. In order to make your dream come true, write down what your dream is, always look to that dream, and imagine yourself achieving it. Also, enjoy yourself while you're at it.

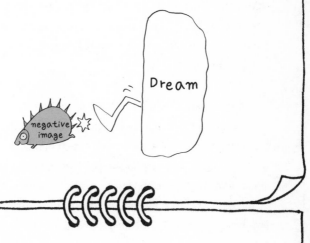

📣 I can do it

1. I will not put limits on my potential. I will aim for a high goal.
2. I will make a list of my dreams(goals) and set medium to long-term plans accordingly, checking them off as I go.
3. I will choose a role model who is successful and will emulate the way that person acts.

The Tide Will Always Come In

This is a story about the "Steel King," Andrew Carnegie.

In the restroom of Carnegie's office hangs a painting. It is neither the work of a famous painter nor a great piece of work. It is simply a picture of a boat with a row lying inside it. However, Carnegie treasured that picture like a jewel. Why was this?

Carnegie came upon the painting when he was a youth with little food or money. The moment he read the caption that the artist had written on the bottom of the painting, Carnegie's heart surged with hope. It said, "The tide is sure to come in. That day I will go out to sea."

Carnegie waited for the tide to come in. He spent many days of his youth cold and hungry, but that piece of writing gave him the power to overcome those hard times. And finally, when he became an internationally known rich man, he bought the painting for a very high price and hung it on his bathroom wall.

The tide will come in for you too. Nurture big dreams and be a firm believer in them. Prepare yourself to go out to sea. Begin right now.

9 *Blessing of the Rainbow 4* |
Believe in Achieving

PSYCHOLOGY OF BELIEF

Believe and roads will clear   Not under any circumstance do I despair; I always believe there is a way.

One day, I arrived back at my research institute after a day of lectures to find one of my chief employees in distress. He told me he needed 80 million won(equivalent to about U.S. $87,000) in a hurry. I asked him when he needed it by and he told me, "by tomorrow." Upon hearing his predicament, I discovered that the situation was quite urgent, and by habit I told myself, 'It's going to work out. God will help.'

That's what I truly believed. Staying calm, I looked for a solution. Suddenly, I remembered Sister J who had recently sold a rice field. Since my mother kept close contact with her, I hurried home and asked my mother if she knew the whereabouts of the money from the sold lot. Unfortunately, the money had been given to the miller as a long-term loan. This was a dilemma, but still I did not despair.

'What should I do?'

I pondered over the matter, and not a minute had passed when the telephone rang. My mother answered the phone and then turned to me and said it was Sister J wanting to pay a visit. I thought to myself, 'What luck!' and signaled to my mother for Sister J to come quick. In approximately 15 minutes, Sister J arrived. I asked again the whereabouts of the money, but the answer was the same; she'd already lent it. On hearing her reply, I sighed and murmured, "What do I do?"

Perhaps feeling pity for me, Sister J asked me, "How much is it you need?"

"About 100 million won(about U.S. $109,000)." I said, thinking I might as well ask for an ample amount.

Sister J thought this over for quite a while before she said, "I'm afraid I don't have as much as that, but if I break open a few of my savings accounts I can make 60 million won."

Then my mother added, "I have about 20 million won."

What a wonder it is to get exactly the 80 million won that was needed. Promptly, I exclaimed, "Oh, thank you Lord!"

At my outcry, Sister J said, "Father, you really should be thankful. It's an odd coincidence that I visited today because the fact is I'm booked for a hemorrhoid operation tomorrow. That's the reason I called today to ask you to pray for me."

It is certain. If you believe, paths will clear. The heavens will help you.

Self-fulfilling Prophecy   Faith is a power in itself. Simply put, we call this the "power of faith". Sociologist Robert Merton created the term 'Self-fulfilling Prophecy' which refers to cases where people's beliefs become reality.

During the Great Depression, when the United States was in economical distress, there was a rumor that a particular bank was about to go bankrupt and customers wouldn't be able to withdraw their money. People who heard the news rushed to the bank to withdraw their cash, and as a result, the bank soon went bankrupt. What the people believed had come true.

Sociologist Min-gyu Lee provides an explanation for self-fulfilling prophecies as the following.

"You will not succeed if you believe such things as, 'I'm not the type to succeed,' or 'I'm not special,' […]

There is one thing you must do if you want to accomplish something. You must strongly deny the belief that, 'I am not talented.' You may have remarkable talent, but it will be of no use if you do not have the firm belief that you have talent. To believe that, 'I am not talented' is fatal."(Min-gyu Lee, Just 1% Will Change Your Life)

The + α from confidence   A famous track star named Charlie Paddock gave a speech at East Tech High School in Cleveland, Ohio, and he said, "What kind of person do you want to be? If you set a goal and believe that God will help you accomplish that goal, it will be sure to come true."

When the speech was over, a young man went up to Charlie Paddock's personal coach and said, "Coach, I've got a dream! I want to be the next Charlie Paddock. I'm going to be the fastest man alive."

At this, the coach said, "It's great to have a dream, son, but to attain your dream, you must build a 'ladder' to it. Here is the 'ladder' to your dreams. It has four 'rungs'. The first rung is determination! And the second rung is dedication! The third rung is discipline! And the fourth rung is attitude!"

Afterwards, the young man made up his mind never to give

up on his dream and finally in 1936, the youth won four gold medals in the Berlin Olympics, later having his name engraved in the U.S. Olympic Hall of Fame. His name was Jesse Owens.

attitude

discipline

dedication

determination

Why did the coach say the highest rung on the ladder is 'attitude'? It is because the way you look at things affect the way you behave, and if you believe in yourself then there is a 'plus α' effect. When belief is combined with prayer, a greater third power which surpasses the 'power of faith' will commence.

EXPECT IT TO HAPPEN

Desire it in Earnest   One day a pupil asked his master how to acquire wisdom. The master did not answer, but simply took the pupil to the river and plunged the pupil's face into the water. The pupil, terrified for his life, kicked and struggled to free himself from his master's grasp, but the master only held on tighter and the pupil flailed his arms and legs even harder. Finally, the master let go of his pupil and pulled him out of the water.

The master asked the pupil, "When your head was in the water, what did you want most earnestly?"

"Master, my only desire was to breathe."

"I am sure it was. Wisdom is just the same. You must desire it most earnestly in order to have it."

What does this story teach us? It is that 'life only gives us what we truly desire.'

Miracles exist On December 16, 2005, there was a fire in an apartment on a residential block in the Bronx, New York. Tracinda Foxe, who was trapped in the building, wrapped her one-month-old baby in a blanket and dropped him out the window. Just at that moment, a man who was a catcher for an amateur baseball team was watching the fire from below and safely caught the infant in his arms.

It was Felix Vazques, a New York City Housing Authority supervisor, who had caught the baby from a 30ft. fall, after which he performed mouth to mouth resuscitation, a skill he picked up as a teenage lifeguard, before handing the infant to rescue workers.

The mother, who was rescued later said, "Just before I dropped my baby out the window, I prayed to God, 'God, please save my son.'" Mother and son were immediately discharged without any injuries after receiving medical attention at the hospital. This amazing incident was reported in the Donga Ilbo under the headline, "Baby Thrown from 3rd Floor Window, Nice Catch!"

Felix Vazques was the ideal person to save this baby's life as he was the catcher for an amateur baseball team and had lifeguard experience. It is truly an uncanny incident. How was it that the apt person was standing below a fire to save a newborn baby's life?

It was a miracle. Amazing phenomena that we cannot explain through reason are what we call miracles.

Act Upon Faith

Speak in 3P sentences 'Conviction' is a strong message as well as a command sent by our conscious to our subconscious. Positive language which is full of conviction eliminates the restrictions that weighs down on your subconscious, and helps you to follow your pursuits without straying from your original path.

Good, affirmative sentences consist of the 3P's: Positive, Present, and Personal. For instance, people generally say, "I won't smoke anymore," but instead, "I am a quitter," is a better way to phrase it.

"I believe I will have the best results no matter what": Say this and act on it. It will bring a positive change to you and the dream you want to achieve, and you will accomplish it.

Act like it has already happened   A man opened a small okonomiyaki(Japanese pancake) shop in the district of Namba of Osaka. However, he had no customers. Several days passed since the opening day, but the shop was still empty.

'What should I do? How will I make people come here?' he thought.

He brooded over his situation, and suddenly one day he put a delivery container on his bicycle and rode around the area in a hurry. He continued this the next day and the next.

People watched the man who raced around town with delivery packages on his bike and they thought, 'Wow! That store must be really popular.' From then on the store began to flow with customers.

Thirty years later, the store became the best okonomiyaki shop in Japan with over 600 employees. The man's name is Masatsugu Nakai.

He is a man who acted busy and made himself the busiest man in Japan.(Kotaro Hisui, Motto Therapy; Finding Happiness in 3Seconds)

The law of achievement is simple. Plan how you will realize what you want, then believe in that plan and act on it.

Act with expectation   This is a story that occurred in a small farming town in the American Midwest:

One year, there was a drought which continued for a very long time. People didn't know what to do. All the crops had dried up and the soil was cracked. Problems became worse and so all the churches of the town united and planned prayer meetings to invoke for rain.

This is what happened at one of the churches: Many people had gathered for the prayer meeting and the church was soon packed. In the very front row sat a little girl. Her cheeks were flushed with excitement, her face glowing like an angel, and laid next to her was a red umbrella. Everyone else had come simply to pray, but the little girl had come to witness God's response.

The little girl's act of bringing an umbrella when asking for rain; this is true faith. Actions that come from faith are altogether different from behavior that sprouts unconsciously and unplanned.

Are we really preparing for what will ensue after we have accomplished what we want? Are we acting with conviction that we have already received what we ask for?

Happiness Guide

Even if you have a dream you must work to realize that dream and have faith in it in order for it to come true. Faith is the 'plus alpha' to having a dream. Faith gives you confidence and the energy you need to work for achievement.

I can do it

1. With confidence I will announce out loud, "My dream will come true!"
2. I will believe in my talents and encourage myself. Having this belief is the most important tool to succeeding.
3. If I want to be a millionaire, I will act like a millionaire. Life only gives us what we truly want.

Faith Cuts through Rock

A man in China was walking the wooded mountains at night when suddenly a tiger came charging at him. In terror, he aimed his bow and shot an arrow at the tiger with all his might. However, the tiger which had an arrow stuck in him didn't flinch. Thinking how odd it was, the man carefully went closer to the tiger and what did he find but a boulder shaped like a tiger!

"My word, I pierced a boulder with an arrow!"

The man was amazed at his feat and once again aimed at the boulder and shot, but the arrow only bounced off the surface.

Like this story, faith is a power in itself. It is a power strong enough to pierce a rock. This is the power of faith.

IV

With All Your Soul: Will Development

To live by putting forth all your soul.
Will development:
this is the secret to experiencing the happiness of
accomplishment.

10 *Find the Blue Ocean in the Corpus Callosum*

CORPUS CALLOSUM, WHERE DETERMINATION DWELLS

Cured from depression after hearing my lectures I have been entrusted with giving a series of TV lectures for PBC(Pyunghwa Broadcasting Corporation) each year for the last few years. I've heard that the ratings are quite high thanks to the fixed audiences for "Water Is Here" and "Treasure Buried in the Field". Other books with the same titles are steady best-sellers, earning love from the general public.

One pleasant surprise from the lectures is that people have reported of being changed after hearing the lectures.

They claim, "My husband was suffering from depression

after he retired, but he watched your TV lectures, waiting for it each time it was on, and now he's much better."

I often hear stories like this. Some people come to my lectures in person and these people all say the same thing: "When I hear you speak, I feel inspired and empowered. That's why I follow you around."

There are various causes and types of depression, but generally depression is a symptom of decreased motivation due to an excess secretion of "sadness hormones". My books and lectures virtually work wonders for people like this. Why? It's because when people hear me speak, endorphins, i.e. 'intracerebral mororphine,' is produced in the brain.

I mainly speak of hope. I offer words of consolation and healing. The words I use most are Gospel, Good News, grace, exciting faith etc. When people hear these words, it is natural for happiness hormones to flow. This is a result of activating the Corpus Callosum, which is the berth for desire.

'The Marshmallow Test' and the Corpus Callosum   Dr. Walter Mischel of Stanford University discovered an astonishing fact from his 'Marshmallow Test'. He took a group of four-year-olds and gave them each a marshmallow, telling them that if they waited and didn't eat the marshmallow for 15 minutes, they would be given another marshmallow.

Of the children who participated in the study, 1/3 couldn't wait the 15 minutes and ate their marshmallows. On the other hand, 2/3 of the children resisted from eating their marshmallows until the 15 minutes were over and was rewarded with another. What was amazing was when the children who were able to resist the temptation of eating their marshmallows had become adolescents, they were able to regulate and control stress and were better able to adapt socially. However, the children who weren't able to endure the 15 minutes had become teens with trouble controlling their emotions.

We all know that endurance is bitter, but the fruit is sweet. The source of this kind of perseverance is determination and the place where determination operates is the Corpus

Callosum. That is why the Corpus Callosum is the third 'blue ocean' which we must pioneer.

CORPUS CALLOSUM, THE BRIDGE OF INTEGRATION

Difference between males and females   Usually females are able to talk faster and in greater quantity than males. What's the secret to this?

The secret lies in the Corpus Callosum. The Corpus Callosum is the bridge between the Left and Right Cerebrum, and this is where reciprocal information exchange takes place. The size of the brain is larger for the male than female, but the tip of the Corpus Callosum is bigger for the female than the male. The back of the Corpus Callosum is called the 'ampullary region'. The male ampulla is shaped like a stick, and the female's is round like a ball. In short, the female's surpasses the male's.

Consequently, this means that the female brain shows better cooperation between the Left and Right Brain than the male brain. Moreover, in examining the operation of the left and right cerebral hemispheres, the female uses both sides of the brain for language, whereas the male uses the Left and Right Brains separately. Therefore, when females think of the spelling of a word they bring into play their emotions and experiences, making females have better command in language skills over males.

In addition, women have a higher capacity to grasp general emotions such as mood or atmosphere, hence appropriately getting rid of stress using multiple emotions, which provides a higher chance for longevity over men.(Daisuke Yamamoto, Reading about the Mysteries of the Brain in 3Days)

This is a great example of how significant the unifying operations of the Corpus Callosum are in our lives.

Unitive perception   A philosopher asked a question to three construction workers who were hard at work:

"What are you doing?"

The worker who was closest to him answered, "I'm laying bricks." The person next to him replied, "I'm raising a wall." But the person farthest away said with great energy, "I'm building a church."

After listening to the three answers, the philosopher surmised the futures of the three men.

"The first person only sees the bricks that are in front of him, so he will lay bricks all his life. The second person can only see as high as the wall, so he will become a factory manager or a technician. However, the third person has immense potential and will be very successful. This is because he already saw the church which has yet to be built."

Anyone is able to see what is immediately in front of him. What we need is the perspective to see the whole. Of course, each element which creates a whole is important too, but you cannot see the whole when you are intent on the thing that is right in front of you. It is like seeing the tree but not being able to see the forest. Bricks and walls cannot bring much meaning to the first two workers. This is why they only concentrated on raising walls with the bricks, but for the last worker, the church was the ultimate goal which he had to accomplish and a final product which would benefit numerous people. That is why he was happy while he worked.

Like so, 'unitive perspective' plays a vital role in weaving together our thoughts with our emotions, and displaying them as action. Integrative ability is closely related to the Corpus Callosum.

The CONDITIONS FOR 21ST CENTURY LEADERSHIP COME FROM THE CORPUS CALLOSUM

Be decisive   There is a dramatic anecdote in the book,

Think and GrowRich, which encapsulates Andrew Carnegie's success theory.

Napolean Hill, who was a novice magazine reporter at the time, went to Carnegie to do an interview on his success story. In those days, Carnegie, who was a magnate in the steel industry and had accumulated enormous wealth, was looking for the right person to complete his success philosophy and had already interviewed over 250 people for the job.

When he met Hill, Carnegie started to test him whether or not he was the right person to finish his success philosophy. "Do you have confidence that you'll see this job to the end?"

Hill replied, "Yes," and Carnegie went on to his next question. "If I give you the opportunity to complete my philosophy, you will have to dedicate twenty years of your life on studying the reasons for failure and success without any monetary compensation. Can you do that?" Hill was shocked, but after thinking over the proposal, he said that he could.

In the interim, Carnegie had been timing 60 seconds on his watch to hear Hill's answer. It had taken Hill 29 seconds to respond. Thus, Carnegie had found the perfect person; someone with a distinct goal, who was decisive, and didn't consider compensation in achieving that goal.

Napoleon Hill received an impressive amount of information from Carnegie, and the book Hill wrote with that information sold over 20 million copies around the world, putting Hill on a seat of wealth. It actually only took four months for Hill to write that book.

Motivation   ·"Whatever you can do or dream you can, begin it. Boldness has genius, power and magic in it."

This is a quote by Goethe. Like his quote, the drive that prompts you to do something at once is no doubt a significant key to happiness and success in life.

A pauper was looking plaintively at the falling rain, worn with hunger. As a gentleman approached, the pauper asked for some alms. The gentleman looked into the eyes of the poor man and asked, "What are you going to do after you fill your stomach?"

"I'll look for a job, I guess. But as you know it's hard to find work these days."

The gentleman then said in a low voice, "What you need is not food, it's that something."

The pauper said brusquely, " 'That something?' What are

you talking about?"

"Something inside you. An ingredient for success. You have something that is more amazing inside you than the potential of what's in an egg. All you have to do is find it and use it."

This shocked the pauper and it changed his life. He went and took the initiative to find work, and ultimately reached an unimaginablely high social position.(Paul J. Meyer's, That Something)

Academic ties, background, health, talent etc. are all helpful conditions to success, but if you don't have 'that something' you cannot succeed. 'That something' is the will inside you that says, 'I will do this, whatever it takes.'

Unyielding determination   People in the Far East plant Chinese Bamboo. They give fertilizer and water to the trees for four years, but the bamboo hardly or don't grow at all. But in the fifth year, the bamboo grows 90 feet in 5 weeks!

If someone witnessed this, they might ask, "This Chinese Bamboo; did it grow 90 feet in 5 weeks, or 90 feet in 5 years?"

The answer of course is, "5 years". If the bamboo did not get fertilizer or water during any period of the 5 years, it would inevitably have died.

Like the Chinese Bamboo, at times our dreams and plans feel like they aren't showing any progress and we're liable to quit. Regardless, people who succeed provide water and fertilizer to their dreams until it comes true. Like these people, if we don't give up, i.e. if we show patience and perseverance, we will be sure to achieve our dreams.

Use the Blue Ocean in the Corpus Callosum

The Corpus Callosum is a vast ocean of choices. This ocean is a 'Blue Ocean,' full of new possibilities where no one has yet cast a net. Use this blue ocean to live a life where all goes well with the next two Blessings of the Rainbow.

– Discipline your language.
– Discipline your habits.

These two principles will be further discussed in Chapter 11 and 12.

Happiness Guide

The Corpus Callosum is a bridge between the Left Brain, which controls reason, and the Right Brain, which controls emotion. The Corpus Callosum also has to do with a person's volition, which is in charge of selection and decision making. In other words, the Corpus Callosum works to unify the brain's functions and to help in achieving your goals. You must govern the kind of language you use and train yourself for a better attitude in order to find the blue ocean in the Corpus Callosum.

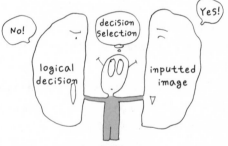

◀€ I can do it

1. I will control my thoughts and feelings, and use them to better my ability in expressing myself. My happiness and success depend on my determination.
2. I will work to realize my dream at once. There are expectations, talent, and power in my boldness.
3. I can't expect things to change in a day. I will work at my goal with unyielding persistence.

Clean the Chamber Pot Well

A funny story remains about the Osan School of Pyeongbuk (now a region of North Korea):

There was a very clever young man who lived in that town. However, he was a servant working in the service of another man's household. This youth came from a poor family and had no choice but to live as a servant, but he was never pessimistic or embarrassed about his situation, but instead he did his work with zeal. He started each day by cleaning his master's chamber pot until it was spick and span. The master watched the youth, who did all his work so sincerely, and thought the youth was too good to be working as a servant. Thus, the master sent the young man to Soongshil School in Pyeongyang and paid for his tuition. He graduated from Soongshil with honors and went back home to teach at Osan School. This young man was one of the Korean independence movement leaders, Man-shik Cho.

Whenever his pupils asked him the key to his accomplishments, he replied, "When it is your time to go out into the world, become a man who washes the chamber pot." This goes the same for us. It means that we should be sincere about the little things.

"Whoever is faithful in small matters will be faithful in large ones; whoever is dishonest in small matters will be dishonest in large ones."(Luke 16:10)

11 *Blessing of the Rainbow 5 |*
Discipline Your Language

THE POWER OF WORDS

Words that have made me   When I was in grade
school, my friends gave me the nickname "Math Wiz"
because I was uncommonly good at math. This name presented me with a unique hobby. In middle school and high school
my hobby was solving difficult math problems.

Another nickname that I frequently heard was "Chadol"
(which means 'quartz' in Korean, but also stands for a 'tough fellow'). Perhaps this is because my last name is Cha or because
I have a dark complexion. Anyhow, it seems people are
reminded of "chadol" when they see me. I feel that this label
has been deeply rooted into my conscious, which is why I'm

always a passionate and steadfast worker.

I still recall what my homeroom teacher said at my elementary school graduation as if it were yesterday.

"Everyone, there are three types of people in this world. The type of person who is useless to this world, the type that doesn't make much difference whether they're here or not, and the type who is needed. I hope you become someone who is needed at school and at home, just like Dong-yup Cha."

It seems the teacher had been quite surprised to see me delivering briquette, with my face smeared black, when he came to make a home visit once. He hadn't dreamed of me, who did quite well in school and was class president, to be delivering briquette! I guess he happened to recall this on our graduation day.

The point is what my teacher said that day stays with me even in the present. Not as an obligation but as joy.

Wisdom of the Talmud   In the Talmud, the Jewish book of wisdom, there is the following story:

A king summoned two jesters and told one of them to find for him the "most evil thing" in the world, and to the other he requested "the good thing" that surpasses any good in the world. Some time passed and the two jesters came to him with their answers. However, they had come up with the same answer. They both responded, "It is the tongue."

As you can see, the tongue can either cause good or it can be lethal.

Words that changed lives   Some years back, the young leader of the Jijon gang in Korea was sentenced to death by the court of law. Before his death he left a speech that oddly stayed with me:

"Seventeen years ago when I was in elementary school, my teacher scolded me harshly for not bringing pastels that we were required to prepare for art class. I was too poor to afford them at the time, but I couldn't bring myself to tell my teacher this. Then, the teacher said, 'Why did you disobey me?' and smacked me.

Later, the teacher said, 'If I tell you to prepare something for class, you should bring it, even if it means you must steal it.' That's when I started to go astray. What that grade school teacher told me changed my whole life. From then on, I started to steal things and I found pleasure in it. As you can see, stealing changed my entire destiny."

We must realize that one wrong word to our children can cause such a horrifying outcome. In particular, the things we tell our young children will immediately take root and become a deep impact on their lives. Words are very powerful.

Language Psychology

Language even affects mold   Dr. Masaru Emoto, a researcher in Japan, studied the effect of a single word using rice. He took samples of a batch of cooked rice, put it into two separate glass jars and wrote "Thank you" on one and "Wretch" on the other. Then he had two elementary school students read the word on each jar, to the jars everyday.

A month elapsed and the results were astounding. The rice which had heard "Thank you" had fermented and had become a rich-scented malt, but the rice which had heard "Wretch" had rotted miserably, turned black, and emitted an offensive stench.

What does this ultimately tell us? The thoughts contained in the language we speak operate as information energy which influences microorganisms. If this is true for microorganisms, it is likely also true for other substances or cells. What is certain is whether it is a microorganism or a certain substance, anything subject to appreciation will present the

"consequence of appreciation," and anything subject to discontent will display the "consequence of discontent."

In this manner, the advice from the Book of Proverbs is significant:

"You will have to live with the consequences of everything you say. What you say can preserve life or destroy it; so you must accept the consequences of your words." (Proverbs 18:20-21)

The key to happiness and misery, success and failure rely on the very words we speak everyday.

Language governs the whole nervous system   Today, the world of neurology accepts as an established theory that the 'speech center' governs the whole nervous system. This means that language can control all the nerves in the body(actions). Consequently, language governs the lives(actions) of human beings.

'Word Therapy' applies this principle in its treatment of patients. In this method, the patient is treated with 'Word Therapy' for an interval of 10-15 minutes, 2-3 times a day. For instance, if the patient has diabetes, that person repeats saying, "My blood sugar level is getting normal," for 10 minutes, and will see excellent results.

Language predicts the future   You can predict a person's future by comprehending the language they use. Success columnist Nae-hwa Lee ascertains this in one of her articles.

"Everyone has been given two things for free. One is 'time' and the other is 'language'. Just as a person's life changes by the way they use their time, a person can either repay a thousand debts, or become an object of loathing depending on how they use words.

Objectively analyze the words you frequently use, and you will be able to predict your future. People who succeed have a different manner of speech.

Start from this question: "How are you?"

When people are asked this they normally answer in three types of categories: the negative, the ordinary, and the positive.

First, the negative. As habit these people answer in the following: 'Not so good.'; 'I'm tired.'; 'Awful.'; 'Don't ask.' ; or 'I could drop dead.'

Second, the ordinary. These people say: 'So so.'; 'Same old, same old.'; 'I'll live.'; or 'I manage.'

Third, the positive. These people talk with zeal and energy: 'Great!'; 'Things are wonderful.'; or 'Everything's going well.'

Of these three types, what type do you find attractive?

The 'successful group' and the 'delinquent group' have different ways of expressing themselves."

People who are positive and use language that promise achievement become what they say and succeed, but people who use negative speech become what they say and fail. In short, our thoughts and then our actions change according to the way we speak, and eventually the words we use become reality.

This is something that happened in France:

There was a politician who was intent on giving his opponent a hard time. Fortunately, he happened to come upon the information that his opponent had come from a background of what was considered a 'lowly' veterinarian career. He stood in front of a room full of assemblymen and announced, "I've been told you used to be a vet. Am I correct?" The other assemblymen grew tense, but his opponent didn't hesitate for a moment and replied,

"That is correct. I am still a veterinarian. Sir, would you like me to take a look at you? You don't look so well."

How dramatic! He reversed the whole situation in a second.

Lincoln also was an adroit speaker. This is a story from his days as a lawyer:

He was defending a young man who was on criminal trial for robbery. Lincoln was sure of his defendant's innocence and said in court,

"According to the defendant's mother, the defendant has never left their farm. In other words, from the day he was born, he has spent his whole life working on the farm. To claim that the defendant committed robbery in a place so far from his home is preposterous."

Thus, the prosecutor immediately countered, "According to the defense, the defendant has not once left his farm since he was born and only did farm work. Then what kind of farm work did the defendant do when he was one-year-old?"

The prosecutor had nitpicked on, "from the day he was born."

However, Lincoln responded without a waver. "The defendant did the milking. Only it wasn't the cow he milked, but his mother."

At this, everyone in the courtroom, as well as the judge, could barely keep from bursting into laughter, and thus, the youth was proclaimed innocent.

WHAT WORDS TO USE

Use words sparingly   Under a stuffed sea bass with a wide open mouth was written,

"I wouldn't be here if I'd kept my mouth shut."

Isn't this a pretty witty remark coming from a sea bass? It's a lesson not to go looking for trouble because of a big mouth. It's quite common for fish and for people to get in a fix for opening one's mouth at the wrong time.

Be cautious when you speak. You cannot take back what is once spoken. What we say has an ability to live and move, so try to use words of commendation.

Use encouraging words

We live off words. The kind of language we hear when we grow up bears different fruit. At a penitentiary in the U.S., 90% of the inmates said their parents told them, "You're going to end up in jail," while they were growing up.

Goethe said, "Treat a man as he appears to be, and you make him worse. But treat a man as if he were what he potentially could be, and you make him what he should be."

Thus, we must always practice hopeful speech. Especially for your children; don't forget that encouraging words are restoratives to them. Here is a poignant example:

Ben Carson, who was director of pediatric neurosurgery at John Hopkins Medical Institutions, was the first person in the world to successfully conduct a separation surgery on conjoined twins.

Also author of, ThinkBig, Carson came from a poor neighborhood and didn't do well in school, but he succeeded in becoming the world's greatest pediatric neurosurgeon and is an inspiration to the young people of today.

Once a reporter asked him, "What made you into the person you are today?"

"It was my mother, Sonja Carson. When I was last in my class and was bullied for being black, my mother didn't fail to give me encouragement and support, she said, 'Ben, you can be anything if you put your mind to it! If you try, you can be anything!'"

Behind great figures like this, there are always words of support which fed and nourished them. Let's think who I might have offered encouraging words to.

Use words of benediction   Language shapes thought, and thought determines action and shapes our lives. This is a result of the automatic nervous system acting on the command of the cerebrum.

What's important here is that the automatic nervous system does not distinguish 'self' from 'other'. If you tell someone, "You're going to do great," "You are an admirable person,"; the automatic nervous system comprehends the words, 'going to do great,' 'admirable,' and you will get into a cheerful state while simultaneously acting in a way which is fit for those words. In other words, it doesn't matter if the subject is 'I' or 'You'. Therefore, if you compliment someone you are blessing yourself as well.

One thing you must remember is bad words influence you under the same principle. If you say, "That's why you can't win," or "What a mess," it's the same as saying this about yourself.

"When you go into a house, say, 'Peace be with you.' If the people in that house welcome you, let your greeting of peace remain; but if they do not welcome you, then take back your greeting."(Mathew 10:12-13)

This is a simple principle. If you bless someone, those words will benefit yourself in the least, and if the other person has the eligibility to be blessed that person will profit too.

Use words of triumph   Boxer Muhammad Ali, who held the reigns of 20th century boxing, is said to have rehearsed each match through speech before going into one. In the world championship against Joe Frazier, Ali said, "I'm going to fly like a butterfly ant sting like a bee." And just like he said, the championship belt was awarded to Ali. Later, as he retired, Ali said that he won half of his victories with his fist, and half with his words. Like so, Ali's assertive way of talking became dauntless messages that could intimidate opponents and was the force that gave him the wings of victory.

The common characteristic among people who succeed is their optimistic and assured way of talking. Even if the end seems out of reach, these people firmly believe success is in their future. If you've lost at a match against someone, or you're caught in a predicament, instead of saying, "I lost," in a defeated tone, try saying, "I lost this time, but I'm going to win next time." Be bold and use words of triumph.

Happiness Guide

Words move and live. Your brain responds to what you say. It cannot distinguish between what is real or not, nor can it determine who or what the subject is. Regardless of whether they are good words or bad words or ordinary words; your future relies on the kind of words you use most often. Therefore, use words in moderation, use words of encouragement, blessing, success, and charm.

◀ I can do it

1. I will praise and commend people more. The things I say will come back to me like a boomerang.
2. I will say things that are positive. My future success and happiness can be predicted by the words I use.
3. I will offer words of hope and encouragement to my family, especially my children. They will grow tall and healthy with those words.

Words that Make me Grow

The poem "Words that Make me Grow" by Sister Hae-in Lee makes us think about the kind of things a person should say in our everyday lives.

When I say, "I am happy,"
I become happy for that moment,
a clear stream runs through my mind.

When I say, "I thank you,"
gratitude bursts anew from my heart,
making me gentle.

When I say, "It is beautiful,"
for a moment I too become beautiful,
and my heart is one shade brighter.

Good words make me grow,
I know this as I speak.

12 *Blessing of the Rainbow 6 |*
Discipline Your Habits

YOUR HABITS BECOME YOUR LIFE

The blessing of dawn awakening   People who are
well aware of the extent of my daily activities occasionally
ask me, "When do you find the time to lecture, do your
research, and write all those books?"

The answer to this indeterminable question is, "Daybreak".
If I secure three to four hours at dawn, this ordinarily substi-
tutes for a whole day's worth of work. This is my secret.

I must confess, "dawn" was a big burden for me. People
say there is the morning person and the late nighter. I felt
going to bed late at night and waking up late was much
more effective when I was student because I'd made this

into my study habit. On top of that, I simply had to finish a book once I picked it up, which meant irregular sleeping hours. However, books on spirituality all preach on the value of evening slumber and using the hours of dawn. I identified with the idea, but still I couldn't resolve to do it myself.

I always had many excuses. When I lecture, it is often that I arrive home after midnight. One day, I suddenly realized that I couldn't go on like this. So, I laid down a few rules. First, I set 10 o'clock as a rule. I went to bed without exception. Then, little by little I got better. My eyes would open at 5, 6 o'clock in the morning. This marvelous development continued. What a wonderful world! If only I'd known earlier!

Power of habit   The following is a short introduction on "me" by an anonymous writer.

"I am the servant of all great people and I'm also the servant of every failure.

As a matter of fact, I am the one who made great people great, but I'm also the one who made failures fail.

Choose me. Discipline me. Treat me strictly. I will make you rule the world. Treat me lightly and I may destroy you."

Who is "I"? You've probably sensed that the answer is 'habit'. This is how powerful habit can be. Aristotle said, "We are what we repeatedly do. Excellence, then, is not an act, but a habit."

'What's learned in the cradle is carried to the grave.' 'A leopard can't change its spots.' 'He that will steal a pin will steal an ox.' These sayings are well-founded. Habits are a manifestation of our everyday lives. They have a great impact on whether or not we succeed. Habits are formed through repetition and they can be eliminated through learning.

However, one thing for sure is that habits are not constituted in a day. The formation of a habit is a process, and it requires a person's endless determination and devotion. A habit that is embedded deep in our bodies, whether it is a good habit or a bad habit is difficult to change. Therefore, we must try our best to cultivate good habits. These things must be taught from "the cradle".

"Teach children how they should live, and they will remember it all their life."(Proverbs 22:6)

A craftsman's disposition born from habit   Long ago, a lord hired a new young gardener. He took close observation of the gardener at work. The youth trimmed every corner of the garden beautifully. Not only that, he even made intricate flower carvings on the wooden pots. The lord, seeing this, asked, "You are not being paid more for carving those flowers on the pots. Why do you devote yourself to this so?"

The young gardener wiped the sweat off his brow with his shirt sleeve and answered, "I love this garden very much. That's why I carve these pots; to make them more beautiful, because I like to whittle. I guess I made a habit of carving flowers on the pots during my spare time."

The lord thought highly of this young gardener and he could see that the young man was talented, so he decided to send the lad to study sculpting. This young gardener later became Italy's greatest sculptor and architect of the Renaissance period. He was the artist, Michelangelo.

Law Of Habit

The Law of Inertia   We subconsciously dislike change. The reason for this is because whether positive or negative, change induces stress. This is a display of our subconscious yearning for stability. Our subconscious reaction is to dislike change and this is called the "law of inertia".

However, the law of inertia, which inclines us to remain in the state of the past, is the key barrier against our making progress.

The "inertia" mentioned here has a negative nuance. On the other hand, 'habit' contains both a positive and negative character. Bad habits become obstacles in life, but valuable habits raises the level of your life and enriches it.

"One, watch your thoughts. You will speak them.

Two, watch what you say. You will enact them.

Three, watch your actions. You will make a habit of them.

Four, watch your habits. They will be your character.

Five, watch your character. It will be your future."

This teaches us that any small thought, word, or action can become a habit, and when it becomes a habit, it will ultimately become your nature and your fate. Habit is not simply the third element in this "life formula". It is the medium that transforms thought into words, words into action, and character into fate. Now, let me introduce to you beneficial "laws of habit" that uses this aforesaid formula in a positive way.

The 21 Rule   In psychology, they say you need 21 days of practice to form a habit. The reason this is called the "21 Rule" is because adults biologically require 14 to 21 days to form a new thinking pattern.

Thus, you must set a distinct goal of the image you want yourself to become, then you must practice this everyday for 21 days, and soon you'll transform into the person you want to be.

There is also the "Rule of 21 Times". This is a rule that you must practice something at least 21 times if you want to make it yours. This rule was a result of an experiment to see how many times a jet pilot must receive mock training to be most effective before being put into war combat, and it turned out that the pilots who were trained at least 21 times had the highest survival rate.

This means that whatever we do, we need to repeat it 21 times in the least. Let's use this "Rule of 21 Times" to form good habits. It takes 21 times for you to make it your own; to acclimate your body to it.

My advice is, if you can, read this book twenty-one times. Then, a miracle will definitely occur.

The Rule of 100 Times   If you happen to be someone who feels you are falling behind everyone else, I recommend "the rule of 100 times". No matter how hard it is, you'll make it if you repeat it 100 times.

An experiment was conducted on leeches. A device was programmed to give the leeches an electric shock when they stuck onto the instrument. The leech, which has no memory, repeats sticking itself onto the device and then falling off, sticking back on and falling off. However, on the 100th time it stops.

The leeches that were used in this experiment had offspring, and those leeches wouldn't attach themselves at all.

Like so, the leech, which has hardly any memory, can learn with 100 tries. If leeches can do it in 100 attempts, there is nothing humans can't accomplish when we repeat something that much.

10-year Rule   Dr. K. Anders Ericsson, professor at Stockholm University and leader in brain research, uses the term "The 10-year Rule" in relation to human habit. "The 10-year Rule" means that in order to arrive at the highest level of achievement in a field, you need at least 10 years of concentrated preparation.

Education psychologist Howard Gardner studied seven creative masters of various fields, who have made great contributions to the world, and came to the following conclusion.

In order to acquire expert knowledge in a field you have to persistently work on it for 10 years. You have to become a complete master in your field if you want to make an innovative accomplishment. We commonly mistake Mozart as an exception from this rule, but he also had to compose numerous pieces of music for ten years before he could produce a succession of great music.

The seven innovators in this study also had to spend 10 years disciplining themselves. Some people needed even more time, and the majority of these figures made another significant contribution after anther 10 years.(Howard Garner, Creating Minds)

Economic expert Byeong-ho Gong says in his book, Creating Master Lives with the 10-year Rule, that achieving success in your profession relies more on how much you upgrade your habits and thinking for ten years rather than your inherent abilities.

Of this, he gives the pianist as an example. Pianists can play the piano without looking at the music, and even if they happen to lose their sight, their fingers move automatically to the right key simply by hearing the first note of a score. This is because their actions have unconsciously been made into habit and those actions are programmed in the brain.

Then, can a pianist be great from the start? The answer is naturally, "No." A pianist needs to be able to move their fingers smoothly between the keys by repeating each new tune repeatedly. Like this, today's habit is created by disciplining yourself until your body moves a certain way unconsciously.

This goes the same for self-image as well. The belief that 'I am this kind of person' is a thinking habit that you have acquired through a long period of time. These mental habits are familiar to you, as if they are the air you breathe or the clothes you wear.

If those self-images are good images that give you joy and help realize your dreams, then there is no problem, but if it's the opposite case then you have to get rid of those mental habits immediately. Be brave and throw away your old mental habits. Then, create new habits and work on them for at least ten years until your new self-image settles in.

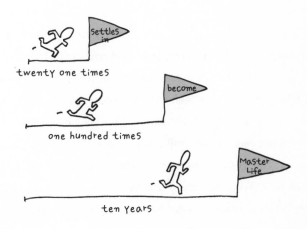

twenty one times

one hundred times

ten years

FORMING GOOD HABITS

What's learned in the cradle can be fixed before we get to the grave   If you want to change your life, you have to change your habits before you reach the grave. A formed habit isn't easy to fix, but with your mental power and persistent effort put into changing your behavior, you can change them.

Of course, it won't be easy, because it takes time for new habits to settle into your body, just like it took time for your old habits to form. Tomio Sato, author of Your Best Life Called to Success, explains the formation of habits as the following.

"New habits can only be yours through the process of persistence, establishment, confidence, and conviction. Therefore, in order to make a conception into a habit, you must think of it often, speak of it often, and write it down frequently, as if you were programming and storing it into your body. As you repeat this process, you will develop the certainty that, 'I can do it!' This is the moment when you have changed the way you think. When you really feel this change in you, you will begin to feel a surge of emotion that, 'I can do it this time too,' 'I can do better.' This is confidence. With the foundation of a confident self, your body will start moving unwittingly, without having to consciously remind yourself to do well. By now, you have arrived at the stage of conviction. Your new habits go through these stages and finally become deeply rooted habits that you are not aware of doing.

Making a new self is to form many new habits on the basis of persistence, establishment, confidence, and conviction.

If you want to be a winner, act like a winner

Steven Spielberg, who at the age of 17 hung around Universal Studios wearing a suit and carrying a briefcase as if he were a professional director, has now become an unrivaled figure in the film industry.

Charlie Chaplin said that you must believe in yourself and think and act like a successful person in order to be successful. "You have to believe in yourself, that's the secret. Even when I was in the orphanage, when I was roaming the street trying to find enough to eat, even then I thought of myself as the greatest actor in the world."

Instead of asking "why" ask "how"

The way to tackle life's adversities is to develop problem solving skills. It is a simple procedure.(Meng Hua Lin(孟華琳), Transforming Yourself in 10 Days)

Instead of asking "why?" ask "how?" When you do this, you will have formed a problem solving pattern before you know it. On the other hand, if you keep asking, "Why?" you're likely to develop a "complaining and dissatisfied habit".

Rather than thinking, 'Why should I do this?' ask yourself, 'How can I use my merits and abilities in this situation?' Or instead of, 'Why is this so hard?' replace the thought with, 'How can I solve this problem?'; 'Why is life so hard?' should be changed to 'How can I give laughter to those around me?' These are the kind of thoughts you should make a habit of.

If you spend your valuable time and effort on complaining about things, eventually the only thing you'll be left with is doubt of your own worthiness. However, asking "how" will provide you with delightful energy, a chance to employ yourself, and it revitalizes your self-confidence, creating a bold and daring attitude.

Success habits   Success is also a habit. There is a saying in soccer that "a person who has the experience of making a goal will be the one to score."

Maxwell Maltz tells us this next story about how to create

"success patterns" in our minds.

There was a salesman working for a printing company, who had the top sales record. He would start each day by visiting his "ally territory". In other words, he would visit places where he knew he would be welcomed. These "territories" were clients he constantly did business with, which meant there would be higher chances that they would order supplies from him without fuss, but even if they didn't buy from him, they would be courteous and he would be treated with hospitality. Only after he visited those places would he go to potential new clients or difficult clients who always wanted to barter. What he wanted was to taste victory before his patience and tenacity was tested.

His boss always said, "Small success brings big success."

It makes sense. These accumulated success experiences form a habit. That is, success is built on top of success. There is nothing quite like the taste of success that makes us succeed.

Let's make a daily habit of success. It can be any kind of success. The more we work at it and the more we make new attempts, the more our energy and passion will grow. Also, as a result, this helps us to accomplish more things. Let's live a life of success through habits of success.

Happiness Guide

Your habits are more important than your natural talents. Small things you practice will become habits, and habits form virtue, and virtue changes your character. Even when you are older you can make a conscious effort to create new good habits.

📣 I can do it

1. I will fix my old habit through training and create a new self-image. I will have faith in the the 21 Rule, the Rule of 100 Times, and the 10-year Rule, and I'll work with tenacity.

2. I will form habits of success for my children and myself. I am already a winner when I've made a habit to work with all my heart, all my soul, and all my strength.

3. Instead of waiting for the "right moment" I will simply begin. My work is half done once I've fixed the habit of procrastination.

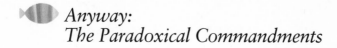

Anyway:
The Paradoxical Commandments

1. People are illogical, unreasonable, and self-centered. Love them anyway.

2. If you do good, people will accuse you of selfish ulterior motives. Do good anyway.

3. If you are successful, you will win false friends and true enemies. Succeed anyway.

4. The good you do today will be forgotten tomorrow. Do good anyway.

5. Honesty and frankness make you vulnerable. Be honest and frank anyway.

6. The biggest men and women with the biggest ideas can be shot down by the smallest men and women with the smallest minds. Think big anyway.

7. People favor under dogs but follow only top dogs. Fight for a few under dogs anyway.

8. What you spend years building may be destroyed overnight. Build anyway.

9. People really need help but may attack you if you do help them. Help people anyway.

10. Give the world the best you have and you'll get kicked in the teeth. Give the world the best you have anyway.

– By Kent M. Keith

V

Healing

There are things that hold us back
even when we try to move on toward our dreams.
In the perilous journey of life
Let's give our tired selves a little time to heal.

13 *Healing of Wounds*

THE DIMENSIONS OF HEALING

Why it's still all right   I've been victim of fraud a few times. I was betrayed because I trusted whatever people told me. Due to this, I've lost the little money that I have, I've lost people, and I've also been wrongly accused. When a person gets conned repeatedly, they are bound to make the conclusion: "I can't trust anybody." Nonetheless, I still have faith in people. Only in this way will the world be a little bit brighter.

Sometimes I believe in people even though I know I'm being swindled. This is the only way people will repent, and through this, I expect they will find a chance to be healed.

Often I am maligned, and at times I am unjustly accused. Some baseless stories about me reach my own ears. Regardless of the kind of work one does, there is bound to be opposition against a person who is assertive. As much as there are people who adore you and say, "I'm a big fan!" there are also people who have opposing views. Before, this used to concern me, but now I'm gradually getting accustomed to it. It's because I acknowledge their difference in opinion, and try to understand their point of view and mentality.

Really, it's still okay! You can avoid being hurt according to how you set your mind to it. Moreover, if you are understanding enough, the wounds you have received can heal on their own.

Words that hurt, words that give strength   People change and are born anew when they are acknowledged by others.

According to a survey, the kind of language that children (in relation to parent/offspring) are most hurt by was, "You're hopeless.(43%)" For parents the most hurtful language was, "What have you done for me?(73%)"; "You embarrass me.(47%)" In other words, children get hurt the most when their parents don't acknowledge them or belittle them, and parents feel most hurt when their children disregard them.

On being asked, "What is most heartening?" children answered that the most encouraging thing to hear from a parent is, "You are the most special person in the world," and parents picked, "I respect you the most."; "I love you."

In addition, husbands chose that they feel encouraged when their wives tell them, "There's no one like you. You're the best." Wives chose, "You're the best thing that ever happened to me."

The survey showed that everybody chose words of acknowledgement as the words that gave them strength. Acknowledgement was what they wanted to hear the most. (Pil Park, Your Words Make Me Happy)

This kind of language is beneficial not only to the person hearing it, but to the mental health of the person who is saying it as well. In fact, when we offer words of encouragement, we ourselves become stimulated which automatically puts smiles on our faces.

Standard of mental health   What do psychiatrists worry about the most when treating a patient? They are most concerned of whether or not it's the right time to discharge a patient.

After much effort, Japanese physician, Dr. Hasao Nakai created the "Standard of Mental Health". If the patient fits into the standards of being "mentally healthy," doctors consider the patient to be cured and allow them to be discharged from the hospital. On utilizing this method, the patients who were discharged under these measurements were later well adjusted to society and not one committed suicide.

Here is a sample of the "Standard of Mental Health".

One. To have the ability to put off something you don't want to do until later.

Two. To have the ability to be by yourself. Also to have the ability to be in the presence of another person.

Three. To have the ability to lie.

Four. To have the ability to compromise at a certain level, and not to be dogmatic.

Five. To have the ability to counter against the feeling that 'no one can do this but me.'(Kotaro Hisui, MottoTherapy; Finding Happiness in 3Seconds)

You might have doubts about these standards. Could these signs really be proof of mental health? The criteria are neither special nor particular. However, if considered the other way around, people who possess these abilities are really the everyday person.

The three dimensions of healing

Many people live with the fetters of fatalism. Fatalism binds a person to their past and annihilates their ideals and dreams.

Up till now, you have been introduced to numerous cases where dreams have come true according to the way one thinks, through language and will. However, in order for these processes to be achieved, you need to overcome yourself. Dreams, hopes, vision can all be realized only when you free yourself from the chains inside you.

Wounds which you have amassed will make you surrender to fatalism. Yet, we humans have the ability to heal those wounds and rise again. Charles de Gaulle's following words are for those of you who are hurt:

"History does not teach fatalism. There are moments when the will of a handful of free men breaks through determinism and opens up new roads."

Then how can we heal our wounds? One of the things which will greatly help in healing our wounds is to comprehend the various dimensions of the human consciousness.

Humans have a conscious and a subconscious. Here, the conscious can be viewed as external healing(or healing of the surface), and the subconscious as internal healing. However, these two cannot be separately treated. The human mind is structured in various layers and because of this it is possible to treat the subconscious by consciously sending positive messages in several directions.

We have the key to change our futures whenever we choose. We can live a life overflowing with joy, good health, happiness, peace, and prosperity. Therefore, if you want to have a healthy positive mind, all you have to do is embrace the messages which correlate to it. You only have to reject the thoughts(intellect), senses(emotion), and action(will) which aren't related to the kind of life you want. The choice is up to you.

Now, in conformity with this insight, we will take a look at the healing of wounds, which corresponds to the 'healing of intellect' and 'emotion'. Then, we will look into the healing of relations, which correlates to the 'healing of will,' and finally we will sum up by studying the healing of self which unifies all three; 'intellect,' 'emotion,' and 'will'.

HEALING OF PERCEPTION

A weak will but strong subconscious Most people think they make decisions solely based on their own intentions, but part of or most of our actions are determined by our subconscious.

'I want to quit smoking, but I can't do it.' 'I want to go on a diet, but I keep craving food.' 'I pledged I would wake up early, but I keep sleeping in.'

We can easily conceive these instances as having a weak will. However, these results come from a foundation of strong subconscious operations. That is, right before we act, the positive subconscious and negative subconscious begin to play tug-of-war inside our heads. And the selected subconscious automatically determines our ultimate action. Recognizing this is the first step to controlling our thoughts.

Then, what can we do? First, we must eliminate the negative images and choose the positive images in our heads. Image is the generative power of the subconscious. Ralf Waldo Emerson said, "A man is what he thinks about all day long." Bear in mind that new images can change the way you think, and your thoughts can change your actions.

The enemy inside me; the White Rabbit   Marco
von Munchhausen in his book, The Little Saboteur: Get
Things Done in Lifeby Conquering Your Weaker Self, refers
to the inner being which blocks you from attempting new
things as "the little saboteur".

Whenever you try to escape your safety zone and step over
the boundaries into your growth zone, a familiar voice inside
you whispers; "It's too hard."; "Do it later."; "You can't
make it."; "Take it easy today." These murmurs are the obstacles keeping you from challenging yourself.

In one of Tolstoy's short stories there is a passage which
reads, "Never think of the white rabbit when you are looking
for the secret to happiness." This refers to a group of children
who hear that the key to happiness is hidden in their yard and
so they go looking for it, but eventually fail because they
keep thinking about a white rabbit.

We all have a "white rabbit". The white rabbit shackles us
with contrary thoughts so that we cannot enjoy happiness and
success. The author of Maximum Achievement, Brian Tracy,
claims the typical "white rabbit" is the excuses which
restrains us, such as 'It's too late for me.'; 'I don't have the

time.'; 'I'm too old for this.'; or 'I can't do anything because of such and such.'

Thus, instead of listing these excuses, we should speak out loud in a clear voice, "I will do this."; "I want to do this."; "I can do this." Then, the subconscious listens to this voice and our misled way of thinking will disappear.

Healing our typical internalized lies   Many people have the misconception that acknowledging their talents is conceit. However, this way of perception keeps us from recognizing our virtues and strengths and ultimately keeps us from self-fulfillment.

Someone who has been hurt immediately acquires a false message; they think, 'I'm not worthy of being looked after or loved.' These thoughts lead the person to self-deprecation.

Dr. Chris Thurman, in his book, The Lies We Believe, argues that a false perception of a certain occurrence leads us to react in a hypersensitive or exaggerated way.

We have to be careful not to show a 5000 dollar reaction when the incident is only worth 5 cents, or to show a 5 cent reaction for something worth 5000 dollars.

He also explains in detail on the 'lies we must confront every minute of our lives.' It is important that we take note of them.

<Self-Lies>

"I must have everyone's love and approval," "It's easier to avoid problems than to face them," "I can't be happy unless things go my way," "Everything is my fault," "Nothing can change," "I'm only going to look at the negative."

<Marital-Lies>

"All my marital problems are my spouse's fault," "If our marriage takes hard work, we must not be right for each other," "My spouse can and should meet all my emotional needs," "My spouse is in debt to me," "My spouse should be like me."

<Worldly-Lies>

"You can have it all," "My worth is determined by my performance," "Life should be easy," "You shouldn't have to wait for what you want," "People are basically good."

<Religious-Lies>

"God's love must be earned," "God hates sins and sinners," "Because I'm Christian, God will protect me from pain and suffering," "It is my Christian duty to meet all the needs of others," "All my problems are caused by my sins," "God can't use me unless I'm spiritually strong."

The first step in healing is to recognize that these lies have pervaded into our perception.

HEALING OF EMOTION

Negative emotions are learned   It is said that over 50 different negative emotions have been identified.

However, they all develop into or are expressed as 'anger,' the core of negative feelings.

Anger is harmful in various ways. When anger implodes, it harms your health, and when it explodes, it harms your relationship with other people.

The most frequently felt negative emotion is doubt and fear, guilt and displeasure. Jealousy is also one of the frequent negative emotions. How are these negative thoughts formed? We learn them when we are growing up through imitation, practice, repetition, and reinforcement. Therefore, because they are learned, we also are able to eliminate them depending on how we handle them.

You may have already guessed that the first place to learn negative emotions is in the home. Once they are learned, people rarely attempt to change those thoughts, saying to themselves, 'I was born this way.' People try to avoid essential questions.

According to Brian Tracy, contrary emotions sprout from two kinds of experiences in our childhood.(Brian Tracy, Maximum Achievement)

First, they come from destructive criticism. If a child grows up hearing things like, "You have a lot of problems," "You can't be trusted," or "You're a liar," that child will definitely accept those criticisms as fact. And they will be recorded once more in the subconscious which will determine future behavior.

Parents reprimand their children's behavior without giving it much thought, simply wanting to fix their child's behavior, but the consequences turn out exactly the opposite of what they intend. Children who receive much criticism while they grow up will later criticize themselves as adults. They are self-deprecating, underestimate themselves, and interpret their experiences in a negative point of view. Even when they have attained great results through hard work, they still feel they are not worthy.

Second, negative feelings come from lack of love. One of the worst things a child can experience is not being loved by either one or both of their parents. Children who grow up like this have a tendency to become emotionally callous or have severe personality disorders.

Strictly speaking, the initial reason we fail in life is because of these negative emotions. Therefore there is nothing more important than getting rid of them.

Apply psychological principles   Though I will discuss the application of psychological principles in greater detail in Chapter 15 on 'Healing of Self,' this method is also effective for 'Healing of Emotion'.

The first method in healing negative emotions is to 'take responsibility.' This begins by repeating, "I am responsible," in a situation or setting where you don't feel good. This simple sentence is quite effective in controlling your mind. The moment you utter these words, you will find yourself calm and rational, and you will be able to look at the situation from an objective viewpoint.

To take responsibility is to become owner of your life, and it is a future-oriented act which helps you find a solution to your troubles. Being angry and spiteful, or critical of others are past-oriented actions which won't help at all when you're looking for an answer.

Another method to healing yourself from negative emotions is to use the "substitute principle". The "substitute principle" is to replace one thought with another because our conscious can only maintain one thought at a time. In other words, we can control our emotions by replacing a negative thought with a positive one. The most powerful tool is to repeat to yourself, "I like myself! I like myself! I like myself!" The more you say these words in a confident voice, the more effective it will be to eliminate negative feelings.

When you cannot control yourself because you are swept away by negative emotions, use the two powerful tools mentioned above. You will find that the deepest wounds have healed.

Vent your anger   Here is a more active means of relieving your anger. You can do this through contact. Dr. Hans Selye found in his studies that physical contact reduces stress.

Selye discovered that we can vent our anger by using four parts of our bodies; hitting with our hands, kicking with our feet, biting with our teeth, and shouting with our voice.

Squash, tennis, golf, baseball, volleyball, and basketball are all sports which require 'hitting'. We can vent our anger from our bodies on the ball by playing these sports.

Sports which require kicking, like soccer, are also effective in venting anger. People will kick anything that comes their way when they are very angry. This is an unconscious act that we do in order to obliterate our rage.

Sometimes we want to chew on something tough. This is

also another sign that we are dissatisfied with something. When we are like this we will feel pacified when we eat foods that need a lot of chewing.

Screaming is another way to vent anger. When you feel small, when you're helpless to do anything about a situation, scream your heart out and you will feel the tightness leaving your chest.

Sometimes you'll see a person hitting or kicking, screaming, or biting when they're in a fight. These are all behaviors to eradicate anger. Sometimes, a relationship with someone will actually get better after you fight them like this. This is because only the good feelings are left after you've eliminated all the bad ones.

Happiness Guide

People are liable to get hurt whether consciously or unconsciously, and these wounds try to shackle you to your past and turn you into a fatalist. Therefore, you have to heal those injuries first in order to free yourself from your fate and greet a new hopeful future.

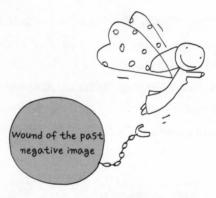

Wound of the past negative image

I can do it

1. I will set straight the false beliefs that I have. I'm going to improve my abilities with confidence.
2. I will acknowledge my responsibility of having negative feelings. Taking responsibility is the starting point to healing.
3. I will transform the sadness and anger inside me into happiness and optimism. I will use this energy as an opportunity for self-improvement.

The Scar That Imprisons the Elephant

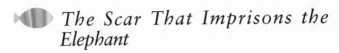

The elephant is the largest living animal on Earth. Even so, they are controlled by humans who don't even amount to 1/10 of their size.

In countries like India or Thailand, people lure young elephants from the wild and shut them in a cage in order to tame them. They fasten a thick chain on the elephant's leg and tie them to the trunk of a large tree. The baby elephant will try with all its might to free itself from the chain, but only in vain. Soon the elephant realizes it cannot free itself after trying and trying again.

Through this process, the elephant loses its will and eventually refrains from any action which surpasses the length of the chain. That is how they won't run away even when they are tied to a tree branch with a flimsy rope after they are fully grown.

Many people become accustomed to the limitations they have acquired for themselves as they grow older. We fear leaving our comfort zone. Will you live like a chained elephant or will you break loose and taste freedom?

14 *Healing of Relations*

THE ONE WHO FORGIVES AND THE ONE WHO DOESN'T

Victim of Unjust Conduct   About twenty years ago, I heard news that a former president of 'Conglomerate X' was suffering from what we call an 'ailment of anger'(roughly translated, it refers to a nervous disorder caused by pent up resentment), and I pondered gravely over the prudence of life.

His story was this:

Anyone who watched the television drama, "The 5th Republic," will recall the incident. During the South Korean 5th Republic, Conglomerate X was completely disjointed due to political machinations. The basis for its annihilation was that the president of X incurred former Korean President Jeon Du-hwan's enmity because X had arrived late to a dinner invitation. Thus, President Jeon Du-hwan had a tax audit conducted on Conglomerate X and confiscated their office building. Afterwards, president of X was unable to get rid of his indignation at losing his building and he fell ill.

This is what I thought when I heard of this:

'To lose a building is a tremendously aggravating event, but it is even worse to lose one's happiness over it.'

Losing a building is not loss of something absolute. However, losing one's motivation in life because of it is.

What would I have done in this situation? I would express my anger for a few days. I would tell whomever I come across about my hurt feelings, I would scream and cuss. However, after a few days, I would calm my fury and tell myself, "Really! Who knew something like this would happen to me? Sure. Nothing's worth more than my life. You'll see. I'll get on my feet again."

The theme in this chapter is 'healing of relations'. That is, in this chapter we are going to examine how to heal the relationships between myself and others. The pith in healing relationships is to 'forgive'.

One small thread   A farmer, 30 years of age, was in the middle of a bustling marketplace when he discovered a piece of thread on the ground. Without any thought, he picked up the thread and put it in his pocket. That day, someone in the market lost his wallet. A person had witnessed the farmer put something in his pocket, so the farmer was charged with the crime and taken away by the police. However, soon the wallet was found and the farmer was released.

Subsequently, the farmer went about complaining on being treated unjustly and declared his rage at the person who had accused him. The farmer couldn't let go of that one piece of thread which was tying him down so that he fell into a state of self-pity, which made him forget all about the farmwork and his family. As a result, the venom of self-pity slowly destroyed him and he died full of rage.

The physical effects of hatred and anger have already been well proven by medical scientists. Although the origin of the farmer's fate was a small incident from a piece of thread, he eventually was eaten by disapproval and anger which turned into self-pity and left him unable to function. If the farmer had accepted the incident as a mere incident and forgiven the accuser, the farmer's life would have been very different.

Forgiveness is for the offender, but it is also for me, to free myself from the resentment and anger inside me. We must practice forgiveness in our lives, even if it is only to maintain our health.

Johann Rist forgives   The musician, Rist, was visiting a certain town. In the hotel lobby, where Rist was staying, was a poster for a musical performance. On seeing the outline of the musician, Rist was surprised to see that he was noted as a pupil of Rist. No matter how hard he tried, Johann Rist could not remember teaching such a pupil. Meanwhile, it came to the attention of the unknown musician that Rist was in town. The musician called on Rist with a face turned white with fear and asked for Rist's forgiveness.

"I am leading a hard life. I can barely make ends meet. I don't even have much musical talent. I thought that I could attain some pupils if I said I was your student. I have wronged you horribly. Please forgive me. I will cancel my recital immediately."

After hearing the musician's apology, Rist asked the musician to play the piano for him.

When he did, Rist corrected him on various parts and said, "Now you are my pupil. So go tell everyone your teacher will be making a guest appearance at your concert. Nonetheless, it

was wrong of you to make a false advertisement that you were my student."

The musician had felt remorse over his wrong and went to Rist to beg for forgiveness. That is why he was forgiven and even received the honor of actually becoming Rist's pupil.

Even Though

To give and discard   The English word, 'forgive' is made up of the words 'for,' which means 'in behalf of,' and 'give' which means 'to bestow'. Pardon is a similar word, and here 'don' comes from the Latin word 'donum,' which means 'gift'. Therefore, to forgive is to give unconditionally, and this is also the Christian spirit.

If God was willing to forgive our mountainous sins, why can't we forgive a meager fault of another? The wrongs we encounter are ant hills compared to what we did to Him.

C. S. Lewis states that it is in the nature of humans to forgive. "To be a Christian means to forgive the inexcusable, because God has foregiven the inexcusable in you."

Even though   In 1983 Pope John Paul II visited Poland, which at the time was tightly veiled from the rest of the world under martial law, and he led a grand-scale outdoor Mass. Crowds of people in groups of diocese walked in procession across the Poniatovsky Bridge and on toward the stadium. Just as they approached the bridge they had to face the main entrance of the Communist Party Headquarters. For hours as the milling crowds passed the building they chanted these words:

"We forgive you. We forgive you."

Some years later, 35-year-old Father Jerzy Popieluszko was found dead with his eyes pulled out and nails torn in the Vistula River. Fr. Popieluszko was greatly extolled for his captivating sermons and people had come in multitudes, filling the church yard, to hear him speak. At his death, once

again Catholics came out to march on the streets with plac-
ards that read, "We forgive you. We forgive you."

The central message of his sermons each Sunday was this:

"Fight for the truth. Conquer evil with good."

Adherents cleaved to his message even after his murder
and it was this spirit of grace which eventually incited the fall
of the communist regime.

HEALING OF RELATIONS

Why you must forgive   Forgiveness is the only way.
There are three reasons for this.

First, if you don't forgive, the anger and hate becomes per-
nicious and will harm you. There are many cases where I've
seen people die untimely as a result of prolonged anger built
up inside them because they do not know how to forgive. Not
all cancer cases are so, but often times, extreme hatred
becomes a source of cancer. The only antitoxin to the poison
of hatred is forgiveness.

According to Dr. Middelmann from Harvard University,
the chances for a heart attack is twice as high for people who
get angry easily than for those who do not. To be angry is to

reduce your life expectancy, and in fact this has been verified by various tests.(Bong-mo Song, The Complacent Human)

Second, you must forgive in order to be free from restraint. The ancient Greek word for 'forgive,' which is the most frequently-used word in the New Testament, means 'to unbind oneself; to set free somewhere far away; to free.' 'Spite' is what keeps our wounds from healing and make us cling to our past, to play it over and over again in our heads, and even when a scab begins to form to heal the wound 'spite' will tear away the scab and open up a fresh wound.

A Rabbi who immigrated to the United States confessed of this: "Before I came to the United States, I had to forgive Adolf Hitler. I didn't want to be holding onto Hitler in a new country."

The initial person to be healed through forgiveness is the forgiver. True forgiveness will free the prisoner, and after you have forgiven, you will realize the prisoner you freed is yourself.

Third, forgiveness is the way to sever the cycle of sin and lead us to the path of coexistence. Only forgiveness will cut the chain of rancor and revenge and let us live in harmony.

Hence Paul the Apostle advised, "Ask God to bless those

who persecute you, yes, ask him to bless, not to curse."
(Romans 12:14)

There exist two heavy burdens until we forgive. One is the heavy burden of the offender and the other is the heavy burden of the offended. Forgiveness frees both from their loads.

Beautiful forgiveness　　　　When a person feels they are forgiven and are freed of guilt, they make a pledge not to do wrong again. Mahatma Gandhi also experienced the grace of forgiveness.

When Gandhi was twelve he stole a coin, and when he was fifteen he stole a piece of gold off his brother's bracelet. He was so eaten up by his guilt that one day he decided to confess his sins to his father. But he was afraid. He wasn't afraid of his father's whip, he was afraid of seeing his father be hurt by a son's wrongdoings. Nevertheless, he had to confess; otherwise he knew he wouldn't be able to get rid of his guilt. He prayed and found the courage to write a confession note. At the end of the letter, he wrote for his father to punish him and please not to get upset for his sake. Then, Gandhi handed the letter to his father who was lying ill in bed. His father quietly sat up and read the letter and soaked it with his tears. A little later, his father tore up the sheet. Through his father's tears and his action of tearing up the letter, Gandhi knew he was forgiven. Gandhi wept too, and from that day forth, he always bore his father's tears and love in his heart and went on to be a great leader.

Happiness Guide

Forgiveness is the central theme in healing of relations. Forgiving is for the benefit of others, but prior to that, it is to free yourself. Forgiving frees you from the anger and enmity that has grown inside you. However, what comes even before forgiveness is to understand where the other person is coming from so that you don't create things to ask forgiveness for.

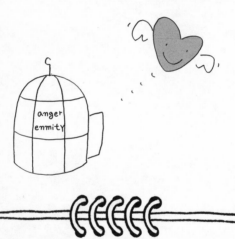

✎ I can do it

1. I will ask for forgiveness if there is someone I have wronged. In this way I will heal myself.
2. I will put myself in another person's shoes and try to understand them instead of getting mad first. In this way I won't have anything to ask forgiveness for in the first place.
3. I will not judge others. There is no one in this world who doesn't make a mistake.

◀▦▶ *Power of forgiveness*

Years ago I saw the movie, "Ben Hur," and a famous scene still remains vivid in my mind.

Ben Hur avenged a most despised foe as he killed him, but afterward the empty feeling he had was indelible and he found himself still holding onto the blade of revenge. One day, when he was roaming the streets of Jerusalem feeling all hollow, he found a youth called Jesus, who had given him water when Ben Hur was being taken away as a slave years back. This time, Jesus was carrying a cross on his back and Ben Hur followed him.

He saw Jesus praying for the soldiers, who had nailed his hands and feet to the cross, "Father, forgive them. They do not know what they are doing." Ben Hur was stupefied. How was it possible for Jesus to pray for someone who had driven nails through his flesh?

That moment, Ben Hur was touched by Jesus' infinite love and mercy, the blade of revenge he had been carrying slipped away from his fingers. And just at that moment, Ben Hur's mother and sister were miraculously cured from leprosy.

This is a very symbolic tale about healing. Our wounds heal when we are deeply touched or when we experience such love which surpasses human limits. This is how mighty the power of forgiveness is.

15 *Healing of Self*

REST

Time for myself   I remember wiping away my tears during the funeral Mass I led for a close friend of mine. He had been a government police officer who frequently had to make overseas business trips. One day, in the middle of the night, I received a phone call to come to the hospital emergency room. He'd had a stroke. I gave him the sacrament of anointing the sick at 4 o'clock in the morning and went back home, but he died later that day. I felt sorry that a man so well known for his meticulous work and serupulous schedule management had his life end so abruptly.

Korea is ranked number one for the death rate of patriarchs dying in their 40's due to overexertion. It is often that we see someone working hard for their family, their company, their country, and then leaving the world unexpectedly. However, isn't it because they choose to overwork themselves? It isn't someone else's story though. I spend many of my "holidays" working.

Why do we rest? Even if it isn't for spiritual or religious reasons, rest is a vital part of our lives. Rest eliminates our fatigue and revitalizes us. To rest is to get into the most comfortable state and unwind. The method is different for everyone; some people sleep, some people enjoy hobbies. Regardless, it is imperative to go through this process. The Right Brain, which manages our emotions, continues to function vigorously even while we relax. When people remain in the state of relaxation for a while, they will often times get a brainstorm of ideas.

Nonetheless, spiritual relaxation is something we can't leave out when discussing rest. Of this Father Thomas Keating said, "The soil of our souls is like hardpan; it does not easily let go of emotional weeds. [⋯] We need the deepest kind of physical and mental rest in order to restore our bodies their natural capacities to evacuate the harmful material that blocks the free flow of grace."

HEALING OF SELF

Three elements of self-concept   "Self-concept"
refers to the belief of self, all of life's territories, and the
world. In other words, the shape we have taken today is a
result of how we construct our "belief of self". We form a
belief system of each realm in our lives and our expectations
and attitudes accordingly determine the outcome.

"Self-concept" consists of three main elements.

The first element is "self-ideal". Self-ideal is the image
you want yourself to become and also the vision to be your
notion's "perfect person". Great accomplishers usually
have a clear self-ideal and advance toward that ideal con-
sistently.

The second element is "self-image". Self-image, which
can also be called the "internal mirror", is directly related to
action. In other words, when you draw a better image of your
self, you will obtain better results.

The last element is "self-esteem". Self-esteem refers to, 'How much I value myself and how much I think I am worthy.' Also it refers to, 'How much I believe I can accomplish something.' In short, it is synonymous to 'self-efficacy'. Tell yourself with passion and conviction, "I love myself! I love myself!" and your self-confidence will get a powerful boost. There's nothing as healthy as loving yourself.

You will reap better results in any endeavor the more you love and respect yourself. Your confidence of your capabilities will grow as well. Consequently, you will make fewer mistakes and become an energetic and innovative person. The same goes for healing of self you have to start by loving and respecting yourself.

Healing from sense of inferiority

At least 95% of the world's population suffers from an inferiority complex, and these inferior thoughts are critical obstacles which block people from living happy and successful lives. However, the truth is this: you are not inferior. This means no one is superior either. We are all just ourselves.

There is only a single individual of "me" in the world; "I am a very special person."

Zacchaeus, chief tax collector of the Roman government, accumulated great wealth by charging excessive taxes and by appropriating portions from taxes collected by other tax collectors. Tax collectors during that time were considered to be deceptive and were regarded with contempt by the Jewish community. Therefore, even though Zacchaeus had become very rich, he couldn't rid of the strange emptiness he felt inside.

One day, Jesus happened to pass through a town called Jericho where Zacchaeus lived. He tried to catch a glimpse of Jesus, but he couldn't see past the crowds of people, so he climbed a sycamore tree to get a good look. Jesus saw Zacchaeus do this, and Jesus said, "Hurry down, Zacchaeus, because I must stay in your house today."(Luke 19:5)

Because of this, Zacchaeus knew that he too had a right to be loved. He healed from his sense of inferiority through Jesus' words and replied in gratefulness, "Listen, sir! I will give half my belongings to the poor, and if I have cheated anyone, I will pay back four times as much."(Luke 19:8)

However, Zacchaeus had another inferiority complex. He was a short man, and he always blamed his ancestors for this. He thought himself to come from a bad line of blood. However, he was, like all other Jews, a descendant of

Abraham, which means he too should be blessed. Jesus made sure Zacchaeus was healed of his emotional injuries. He said, "Salvation has come to this house today, for this man, also, is a descendant of Abraham. The Son of Man came to seek and to save the lost."(Luke 19:9-10)

Zacchaeus was so short he had to climb a tree in order to see Jesus, but he was able to become a truly big person through his meeting with Jesus.

Healing from guilt

'Guilt' is the same as 'having a tormented conscience'. In other words, guilt and conscience go hand in hand. The conscience is what instigates feelings of guilt when we act against the ethics or rules we have learned to abide by, and the guilt leads us to the right path.

Of course it's a problem if you feel too much guilt or don't feel any guilt at all when you've clearly done something wrong, but an adequate amount of guilt is an internal warning system which exposes the sins we have committed in our lives and shows us how far away from God we have wandered.

Judas and Peter both betrayed their master Jesus Christ, but Peter later became a founding figure in the Catholic Church, whereas Judas hung himself from a tree and committed suicide. What was their difference?

What happened was Judas wasn't able to forgive himself. Peter, on the other hand, forgave himself after much contrition, and by forgiving himself he was able to have the strength to convey his Master's words to others even under religious persecution. When he was sentenced to execution, he said, "I have betrayed my Lord, so I shall die upside-down on a cross," and chose a noble death.

Judas had gone to the high priests and threw the 30 silver coins at them, with which he had bargained his Master's life. He had most certainly realized his wrong and was enraged at his own doings and the high priests who had incited him to do such an act, but he did not forgive himself.

Peter and Judas both lamented and repented, but because one of them couldn't forgive himself, his life ended with suicide.(Ho-seung Jeong, The One Word That Changed My Life)

How different they were! We will be freed from the burden of guilt once we wash ourselves of misled guilt.

Healing from sense of defeat   There are times when we fail even though we put our best efforts into achieving a goal. No one makes the right decision all the time; we all make wrong decisions every day of our lives. It's only natural.

At no costs should you blame yourself or be self-deprecating for mistakes or failures you have made in the past. The important thing is to plan a new tomorrow and to find what you can do now. It's essential to find what you can do by reevaluating your goals, instead of regretting what you could not do. People who are overly critical of themselves find it difficult to go onto new things.

Behind every successful person is a trail of even more failure. Baseball legend, Babe Ruth hit a grand total of 714 homeruns, but in order to get to that number he had to taste the bitterness of 1,330 strike outs.

Do not feel hurt because you have failed. Accept your defeat as is, because it's the only way you will rise up past it.

The Primary Road To Healing

'I am responsible'   The most powerful cure which can be used for all types of healing is to have a responsible attitude. Brian Tracy said the key to healing is taking responsibility.(Brian Tracy, Maximum Achievement)

If you take a deeper look; responsibility = self control = freedom = positive attitude. On the other hand, irresponsibility = loss of self control = restraint = negative attitude. Take a close look at your inner state. You will be surprised at how accurate these equations are. Once you realize this, you will easily be liberated from negative perceptions of yourself.

People who are responsible are usually optimistic and self-confident. However, irresponsible people are pessimistic, have a tendency toward defeatism, and are sarcastic. They also have low self-esteem and don't have goals. This is because taking responsibility is a future-oriented act, but to be angry and resent someone or to look for someone to be critical of is a past-oriented act.

Therefore responsibility contains in it both freedom and an ability to control. This causes us to feel very optimistic and ambitious. In short, we become happier the more we accept our responsibilities. However, having an irresponsible attitude, to feel you don't have control over your life because of this and to feel lack of freedom instigates unhappiness, anger, and frustration.

Frankly, the starting point of any decision begins with you. Most people hate and resent people who have wronged them, but to be exact, this is a way of avoiding responsibility. You have been afflicted because you made that certain decision. To be responsible is to accept that fact.

Therefore, we must be more actively aware and comprehensive about our situation. An effective method to do this is the "substitution principle". The substitution principle is to replace negative thoughts with positive thoughts. Our conscious can only think of one thing at a time, and we are able to consciously select what we are going to think about. Thus, all you have to do is push out your negative thoughts and substitute them with positive ones.

"I am responsible." This is a very effectual sentence in healing the self. The moment we say these words, we become calm and rational and we are able to see the situation from a clearer viewpoint.

To go a step further, you should sincerely empathize and console someone who comes to you in distress, but then later let him/her realize that the person responsible for the problem is him/herself. The attitude that you will take 100% responsibility for your life, this is the key point and also the starting point in healing the self.

Have 'inverse paranoia'   People who have a healthy self-image are always full of confidence and think the best of their situation. They also hardly despair about an outcome.

This is because their belief in themselves has the ability to win over any negative doubt. They expect the most beneficial out of any kind of circumstance and charge their whole surroundings with positive energy.

The basis for a positive attitude is to have "inverse paranoia".

"Inverse paranoia" is to have the belief that the world is leading you toward happiness and success. 'Something wonderful is going to happen to me today.' Like this, a person always expects the best for oneself.

Victor Frankl, famous also for "logotherapy," once received a phone call at 2 o'clock in the morning and a low woman's voice could be heard on the other end of the line.

"Are you the famous psychologist, Victor Frankl?"

"Yes, this is he⋯."

"I'm sorry to call at such a late hour, but I just don't have the strength to go on. I have a handful of pills. I'm going to die now."

Frankl hurriedly tried to persuade the woman out of it. "There is no reason to kill yourself," "If you try with all your might, there's nothing you can't accomplish." He tried to convince the woman with these types of condolences.

The woman talked with him for quite some time and said she would follow his suggestion and put off her attempt for now on condition that he meet her right away. Frankl conceded and waited for her arrival full of curiosity. What had he said that made her decide against taking her life?

The woman upon meeting Frankl said this:

"I can't remember a word you said to me, but the reason I changed my mind was because even though a woman you've never seen in your life called you in the middle of the night and complained about her life, you didn't show any sign of annoyance and you were sincere about trying to help me. I thought that if there are people like you in this world, it just might be worth living."

The moment you find meaning in life, no matter how trivial it may be, that much of your afflicted self will be healed.

Happiness Guide

Healing of self begins the moment you love and respect your-self. But you need to go a step farther and accept responsibility. Only then can the most inner core of your soul be healed. Then you will mature and flourish. Only then can you love others as well.

◀ I can do it

1. I will regularly make time for my soul to rest and be purified. When my soul is purified and rejuvenated my life will get back into order.
2. The means to healing my self-image is to accept responsibility and love myself the way I am. I'm going to give myself a warm hug when I've made a mistake.
3. I will try various methods of healing and find what works for me; being more responsible, having a positive attitude, finding something meaningful, broadening my scope of understand-ing, and having hope.

Even if silent

Cardinal Kim Su-hwan found a poem written on the wall of a bomb shelter while he was in Cologne, Germany.

Though the sun is hidden behind the clouds,
I believe there is a sun.
Though I cannot feel a drop of love around me,
I believe in love.
Though God remains silent,
I believe He is here.

Think how this person must have been consoled by writing this verse at the time. How many times he must have evaded death during the Nazi regime. Also his inner clouds of despair were probably healed.

VI

Life Vision

What makes your heart race?
Isn't there a life vision that will make your heart race
even if you were to pursue it your whole life?

16 *Pursue a Goal in Life*

WHY IT'S IMPORTANT TO HAVE GOALS

Goals let you elude death   While I was studying in
Vienna, there came an occasion where I had to go to
Innsbruck with a few friends. All four of us drove in one
car. There was the owner of the car, her son, another student from Korea, and myself. On the ride home, the car
suddenly swerved, hit the guardrail and flew into the air,
rolling three times and finally coming to a stop. It was like
a thrilling stunt you can only see in the movies, and while
the car was turning in the air, only one thought flashed
across my mind:

'But I still have something left to do.'

The car came to a stop upside-down. The cause of the car accident was a flat tire. One after another, we checked on each other and found that everyone had survived. I was the last one to unfasten my seatbelt and climb out the window, which was smashed to bits. Outside of the car, I discovered the crank snapped apart and the body of the car totally crushed. I looked around and found that the toolbox, which was initially in the trunk, had crashed through the window and was lying far from the scene. 'What if the toolbox hadn't made it out the window and hit someone in the car?' I thought.

Another miracle was the fact that I had been sitting in the front passenger seat. Originally, my seat was in the back where a seatbelt was missing, but on the way back from Innsbruck the Korean student who had been taking turns driving said he wanted to sit in the back and get a little rest. "Then why don't we change seats till the next resting area?" and we'd changed seats.

This student was a brawny guy who had a thick neck like Mike Tyson. Right after the accident, he said, "I just grabbed onto the front seat with both hands when the car started to roll."

His neck was splintered and he had to wear a cast for a while, but if we hadn't swapped places, I would have definitely died on the spot.

The next day, a photo of the crushed automobile made the front page of a local newspaper. The caption beneath the photo read, "Miracle: Four People Survive."

I still have that picture. It reminds me of what I should focus on while I'm alive. I am still convinced. The thing that saved me that day was the thought which had struck my mind, 'But I still have something left to do. It's not my time.'

Yes, there's something I have to do. This is the stimulus that drives me forward every single day.

Story of a native Saharan

There is a small village referred to as the 'heart of Sahara' in the West Sahara Desert. Every year many tourists go to the Sahara in order to visit this town. However, before a man named Levin discovered this place, the village was isolated from the rest of the world. No one in this village had gone beyond the desert. Many people tried to flee this barren land, but not one succeeded.

Levin asked these people, the best way he could, using body language, why they couldn't get past the village. Everyone had the same answer.

"No matter what direction I take, I end up at the same place where I started."

Levin wanted to see for himself whether this was true and headed out toward the north. He got out of the desert in three days. Then why couldn't the villagers do so?

This time, the frustrated Levin accompanied a village youth to see what would happen. Ten days passed. They walked night and day, but on the 11th day they ended up back at the village, just as the villagers had told him. Levin finally discovered the reason why these people could not get past the desert. They had no knowledge of the North Star.

Levin then took the aforesaid youth and went on another journey. This time, he made sure they rested sufficiently during the day to save their energy and walked at night following the glow of the North Star. This way, Levin taught the lad how to get past the desert. The youth did as he was instructed, and indeed, they reached the end of the desert within three days. The youth later became a pioneer of the Sahara, and in the center of the pioneered land stands his statue. At the bottom of the statue these words are engraved:

"A new life begins when one finds their direction."

Regardless of age, true life's journey begins the moment a person sets a goal, and the days before this are simply trivial.

Everyone needs their own North Star to guide them through the journey of life.

DISCOVERING YOUR PURPOSE IN LIFE

Terminal values and instrumental values   Values can be divided into "terminal values" and "instrumental values". "Terminal Values" refer to values where the values themselves are the end such as equality, social justice, and peace. "Instrumental values" are values which are used as tools to an end, like honesty, responsibility, and forgiveness. There are also values that can either be terminal values or instrumental values such as money or religion.

However, it is when an instrumental value is misinterpreted as a terminal value that the misery starts. Suppose your aim is to earn a lot of money. After you have reached that aim, you will find yourself feeling little pleasure, but if you use "earning a lot of money" as an instrumental value, and say your terminal value is to use that money for good deeds like charity, you will truly feel fulfillment in life.

There are numerous self-help books on the market declaring they will help you find purpose in life, but the one thing these books have in common is that they emphasize "instrumental values". 'Think what your dream might be.'; 'Establish a vision.'; 'Find what you're good at.'; 'Work to accomplish your dream.'; 'Persistently discipline yourself.'; 'Believe in your vision.' The list goes on.

Of course there are many cases where people realize success by following this sort of advice. Generally, people will successfully arrive at the end of their goals if they devote their hearts and souls into it. However, it is one thing to accomplish one's goal and another to fulfill a life purpose. We need something more than the suggestions in these self-help books.

"For if you want to save your own life, you will lose it; but if you lose your life for my sake, you will find it."(Mathew 16:25)

Instrumental values are simply instrumental values. Money, fame, and social status are only a means of attaining happiness, peace, salvation, and gratification.

Searching for a purpose in life   Then what should we seek in life?

During the first half of the 20th century, several inquiries were made into the purpose humans pursue by the Vienna Psychoanalytic Society. Austria as the birthplace of psychoanalysis, the Viennese School consisted of the First Viennese School of Sigmund Freud, the Second Viennese School of Alfred Adler, and the Third Viennese School of Viktor Franl.

Father of psychoanalysis, Sigmund Freud espoused the idea that humans are pleasure-seeking beings. Freud's "pleasure" refers to sexual pleasure and he claimed sexual desire is the fundamental human desire, and without this, humans lose ego, i.e. self. When sexual desire is fulfilled, people find their ego and thus attain happiness. Reversely, when sexual desire is suppressed people become unhappy. Freud's argument consequently voices that people live in order to fulfill their physiological desires. In other words, his logic is that people can attain happiness once they satisfy their need for eating, sleeping(shelter), and sex.

On the one hand, Alfred Adler declared on the limitations of Freud's theories. He embraced Freud's assertion on the human 'will to pleasure,' but Adler added that in the depths of human psychology humans have a 'will to power'. According to Adler, humans socialize, pour all their energy into their work, try to prove their competence, and aim to go "higher" because we have a 'will to power'. Therefore, he maintained that people find happiness when they attain more power. In fact, Adler's adherents are putting all their effort into gaining triumph in the intense social power game even at this minute.

Viktor Frankl went a step further and declared that the basic human desire is a 'will to meaning'. Humans are beings who pursue meaning, and it is true that humans have a will to pleasure and a will to power, but the most basic and central desire is a will to meaning. Thus, even if the two wills to pleasure and power are met, people will not be happy unless this particular desire is fulfilled. However, even if the will to power and pleasure are not gratified, people can find happiness if the desire for meaning is satisfied.

What is "meaning"? It refers to finding one's existence worthwhile in the relationship with others. The thought that 'I am important to someone,' that 'I play an important part in someone's life' all help in finding meaning.

What should we pursue in life?

Whichever road we choose to take, our lives will look the same from the outside. It even takes the same amount of work. But the quality of life, the inner bliss, will either be like heaven or earth depending on which road we take.

LIFE WITH A MISSION

99% and 1%   Masanori Kanda, one of the best business consultants in Japan, who has enlightened over 10,000 CEO's with his success strategy, said this:

"Calculate backwards from your future and decide what you will do today."

99% of people predict what the future holds by looking at their present, but only 1% looks to their futures to decide how they will act now. Needless to say, people belonging to the 1% are the ones who succeed. And the majority of people say they can't understand the 1%.(Kotaro Hisui, Motto Therapy; Finding Happiness in 3Seconds)

1% of the world thinks of their futures while they live in the present. This means they think of what they must do today in order to attain the picture they have drawn of their futures.

The 5 Step System to achieving your goal

You need a proper method in order to achieve your goal. The following 5 Step System is a concrete plan in which the Blessing of the Rainbow has been implemented. The Blessing of the Rainbow is not a technical or simple prescription that previous self help books have offered. It is a fundamental, unitive system. It is a manual to help anyone reach their goals and dreams through practice and repetition.

The Blessing of the Rainbow can be applied a little differently according to each personal case. In other words you can mix and match to fit your own plans. If the main plan is to accomplish a goal, The Blessing of the Rainbow can be transformed into a five step system like the following. Then let's take a look at how this goal accomplishing system works.

Step 1: Have a strong wish.

To wish for something in earnest is the basic attitude that you must have when you have a goal. Wishing gives you motive, and it helps move you forward against any obstacle. This corresponds to the 3rd Blessing of the Rainbow, 'Nurture a dream.'

All your dreams and hopes depend on your ability to set a goal and act on it. To put it another way, goals play an important role in having a happy and successful life. So many more people would set goals if they only realized this. They would live a more wholesome life.

If two people are set side by side in an experiment, who have similar backgrounds, intelligence, education, and experience, the person with the stronger sense of purpose will always do better.

What does this mean? It means people without goals are destined to work for the people with sure goals.

Based on the SMART rules mentioned prior, having a specific goal raises your chances of accomplishing it, and this can be solidified when you write down your goal on paper. Sadly, there are few people with sure goals. Less than 3% have their goal written on paper, and less than 1% record and check on their goals on a regular basis.(Brian Tracy, Maximum Achievement)

Write the goal you want to accomplish and write why you want it. This is an important process in giving your wish shape and making it into reality.

Step 2: Have firm faith.

If you don't believe, you cannot achieve. This is congruous to the 4th Blessing of the Rainbow, 'Believe in achieving.' The stronger your faith is that you will accomplish your goal, the higher the chances are that you will make it. Belief creates actions to fit that belief and propels you to keepgoing forward toward your goal. Eventually, a strong belief that 'what I want I will get' will become a reality in itself.

The 1st Blessing of the Rainbow, 'Think positively,' is what will solidify your belief. That is, when you have "absolute optimism" that you have the competence to accomplish your goal and that it will be achieved no matter what; this is when your faith becomes definite.

Step 3: Use "achievement language".

When you have acquired a firm belief in yourself, then I advise you to express this in "achievement language". Positive language helps you drive you to your goal. This goes under the 5th Blessing of the Rainbow, 'Discipline your language.'

Prior, we have learned that 3P sentences are what settle into our subconscious and produces great impact on us. That is, the importance of Positive, Present tense, and Personal sentences. Use this rule and repeat sentences everyday such as "I am a goal achiever," "I am already such and such," or "My salary is such and such."

Step 4: Act with "achievement habits".

Now we have to go beyond words and plunge into action. In order to act persistently toward your goal, you have to adapt "achievement habits". This is connected to the 6th Blessing of the Rainbow, 'Discipline your habits.' Among various habits, here are some useful ones I would like to offer you.

First, you need a 'habit of gathering information'. This habit refers to making a habit of creating a list of all the knowledge, talents, techniques, abilities, and experiences you need in order to accomplish your goal and finding out what kind of information or technical skills you need for it, then learn those skills or knowledge as soon as possible. This method corresponds with the 2nd Blessing of the Rainbow, 'Scatter the seed of wisdom.'

The next important thing is to create a 'habit of planning'. First, figure out where you are currently and set a method and deadline to act on it. This habit is closely related to all the elements of the SMART rule mentioned previously. What you must bear in mind is to improve your plans as you put them to practice. This is because thorough examination and feedback drastically raises your goal achievement potential.

Finally, there is the 'habit of visualization'. This refers to imagining a clear vision of yourself after you have already accomplished your goal. The more you picture this the more your desire of accomplishment will grow, and your belief will get stronger. This is one of the methods in the 3rd Blessing of the Rainbow, 'Nurture a dream.'

Step 5: Never give up.

If there are no obstacles when you are advancing toward your goal, then this is not a goal, but just a mundane day. Don't think of the possibility of failure. Never give up mid way. If you stay with it, you will eventually achieve your goal. Goals start with wishes and are completed with tenacity. This is congruent to the 7th Blessing of the Rainbow, 'Never give up.'

Accomplish "small goals" first

When do people most feel they are incompetent? It's right after they have come upon an obstacle and failed at something. Speculating, 'How will I get over this?' when one fails, simply lowers your self-esteem.

Instead of attempting to get to the top overnight, let's set "smaller" goals first. The small pleasures in achieving little things are not only good for your mental health, but it's a shortcut in regaining your self-esteem.

There was a marathoner who came in first place in each marathon he ran. People said he was a born runner and exclaimed at his feat.

Like always, he came in first in another marathon, and a reporter asked him, "Marathons demand such extensive long-distance running. I expect it's much easier to get exhausted running a marathon than any other running event. What's your secret to be the first to cross the finish line every time?"

The runner laughed and said, "It's a very simple method. I divide the total running distance into stages. When I finish the first stage, I cheer myself on, 'Okay, I made it through the first stage! Now, let's take on the next stage!' If I think of how I've succeeded past each stage, I don't get tired as much. Before I know it, I'm at the finish line."

Happiness Guide

A person with purpose can persevere through any hardship and find value in it because they concentrate only on the purpose in their life. You must set terminal values as your goals, such as justice, peace and happiness, and use instrumental values, such as fame, power and wealth, for the means of reaching your goals. It is important to set specific goals and achieve them step by step.

🔊 I can do it

1. I will set a clear goal. I will write a mission statement about what I will devote my life to.
2. I will set 'procedure goals' in order to arrive at my ultimate goal. I will make a list of specific, step-by-step goals.
3. I will pursue my purpose and goals not out of duty, but with pleasure. If there is something I have to do, I will have fun doing it.

Purpose shines through during crisis

Little more than a hundred years ago, there was a conflagration that swept over Chicago. When nearly everyone bemoaned their loss, there was one store that put up a sign reading,

"Our shop has completely burned in the fire, but our purpose has not. So tomorrow we're doing business as usual."

Purpose shines through at times of trouble. If you throw away your purpose because you've come upon hard times, then it's not real purpose. Although you might be skipping meals and your shabby house is falling apart, if you have purpose, the light of hope is still burning.

17 *Blessing of the Rainbow 7* |
Never Give Up

HISTORICAL LESSONS

Just 5 meters more   I once climbed the Alps while I was studying abroad in Vienna. At arriving at the peak of the mountain, I found a lodge, and about 5 yards from the lodge was a cross. The story of that cross goes like this:

A mountain climber met a severe blizzard on his way up the Alps. He knew there was a lodge at the summit, so he went forth trying to get to the top of the mountain through the snowstorm. However, to make conditions worse, soon the sun set and darkness swept over. He plowed through the darkness and driving snow which was getting harsher by the minute, but there was no lodge. Not able to see more than a few feet ahead of him, he started to think he was lost and fell into despair. Eventually, he gave up and collapsed on the spot.

The next day, after the storm had lifted, people discovered a mountain climber who had frozen to death on the side of the trail. The location where he had died was only 5 yards away from the lodge.

If he had gone five more yards through the darkness and snow, he could have lived, but he had fallen into despair and given up.

After hearing his story, I tell myself whenever I find myself in hardship:

"Just five more yards!"

A story of a masterpiece   Cervantes was 53-years-old when he wrote this book. Everything he did before this had failed. At last, he found employment as a low-rank government employee, but even this ended with him being fired. As these instances recurred, Cervantes lost self-confidence. Moreover, the wound on his left hand from the war made him even more depressed.

One day, he was imprisoned for a slight mishap, and he considered this to be the end of his tragic life. But he found a burning ambition for writing while he was in prison. When the manuscript was introduced in the form of a published book, the public raved.

This piece of work has been read by people all over the world for over 400 years. It is DonQuixote. The name of the author to find opportunity in time of difficulty is Miguelde Cervantes. Humanity cannot be broken, regardless how difficult circumstances maybe.

LOOK FROM UP HIGH

Trust in Providence   Eagles are not born with the ability to soar through the air, nor do they know how to use their sharp beaks or eyes from the beginning. The mother bird trains her young so that they become strong birds of prey. (Gwan-ho Na, Nothing I Can Do but Win)

The eagle's nest is on the edge of a high cliff. When it is time, the mother bird shakes the nest and pecks at the young eagles until they fall off the cliff. The young birds screech and flap their wings awkwardly as they fall, and just when they are about to hit the ground, the mother bird swoops to the rescue and lifts them up with her wings. The mother bird repeats this until they are able to fly on their own. The young eagles learn how to fly through this process. Finally, another fearless eagle is born.

God's love is just like the love of the mother eagle.

He turns evil into good   The story of Joseph in the Old Testament is touching. He was the 11th son among the 12sons of Jacob. But Jacob loved Joseph more than any of his other sons because Joseph was the first son to be borne by his beloved Rachel. As a result, Joseph was rejected by his brothers until at last his brothers banded together and sold him as a slave to Egypt.

In the interim, Joseph was met with many trials in Egypt, but by interpreting the pharaoh's dreams, he made Egypt prepare for the drought which was to last for seven years, and became second place next to the pharaoh.

When the severe drought came, Joseph's brothers went to Egypt looking for food, and after many complications met their younger brother, Joseph.

However, the brothers feared a reprisal from Joseph for the ill they had committed. Nonetheless, Joseph wasn't as petty as they thought. Because Joseph believed in the Lord's foresight, he forgave his brothers and said, "You plotted evil against me, but God turned it into good." (Genesis 50:20)

This goes the same for us. Do not despair no matter how adverse your situation is. Instead, look forward to something even better that will come through that adversity.

NEVER GIVE UP

Courage to start over whenever that may be "A pessimist sees the difficulty in every opportunity; an optimist sees the opportunity in every difficulty."

These are the words of Winston Churchill. It's true. Let's take a look at this true story which demonstrates this dictum.

In December of 1914, there was a great fire in the laboratories of Thomas Edison in New Jersey. Due to this incident, experimental equipment worth millions of dollars was lost along with Tomas Edison's journals, which he had devoted his whole life to. The next morning, seeing his laboratory, which had contained his entire hopes and dreams, turned to a pile of ash, he said, "There's great value in disaster because all of our mistakes are burned out. Thank God we can start again!"

And he started his research once again. Edison was 67 at the time. In spite of the misfortune which had come his way, he maintained his determined and goal-oriented attitude. Because of this, he was able to avoid misery even when he had lost everything.

You simply haven't met your time   One of
Lincoln's quotes is, "I have been driven many times to my
knees by the overwhelming conviction that I had nowhere to
go. My own wisdom, and that of all about me, seemed insuf-
ficient for the day."

Lincoln experienced numerous failures before he was hon-
ored with the position of President. In 1816, family bankrupt-
cy, his business failed in 1831, he ran for Congress and lost in
1832, business failed again in 1833, fiancee died in 1834, was
hospitalized from a nervous breakdown 1836, in 1843 and
1848 lost both times in the race for Representative, and in
1854 and 1858 lost both times in the race for Senator. Each
time he failed like this the temptations of despair lured him.
Fear swooped down on him. But he didn't give in. Finally, he
overcame failure and fear, and in 1860 became the President
of the United States.

We are free to choose between resigning to failure and
defying it, fretting over our failure and ignoring that anxiety
and moving forward.

Still great after failure   To commemorate the end of the 20th century, BBC selected the 'top ten explorers of the century'. Among them, Ernest Shackleton caught people's attention. He was the hero of the "Endurance Expedition" credited for being "a failure even greater than success".

In August 1914, Ernest Shackleton and his crew of 27 men started off on the world's first trans-Antarctic expedition. However, 150 km from his destination the ship got trapped in ice and subsequently the ship sunk. He and his team barely managed to travel across one floe to another and eventually Shackleton chose five men to take the life-risking escape route to safety. This route was the first ever successfully made. Finally, two years after the expedition had begun; he was able to bring back all his men alive.

What had made those men survive? It was the determination that Shackleton had to never give up as long as they were alive.

Edmund Hillary, who was the first man to conquer Mount Everest, said of Shackleton, "When disaster strikes and all hope is gone, get down on your knees and pray for Shackleton."

Although he didn't succeed in his first goal to cross the Antarctic, he did succeed in saving the lives of his men, which is what people applaud him for as "a great explorer," "the best leader," and "a hero who thought of his men first".

His failure was not simply a failure. It was a failure that shined brighter than success.

A life that knows not how to give up   Churchill gave a commencement speech at Oxford University. He appeared at the ceremonial hall in a stately manner, a cigarette between his lips. Churchill received wild applause and slowly he took off his hat and placed it on the podium along with his cigarette. The audience held their breaths and waited for a stunning speech.

Finally, he opened his mouth, "Never give up!" He said the

first powerful words, and then he turned his head slowly looking at everyone in the audience. Everyone waited to hear his next words, and he said, "Never, Never, Never, Never, Never, Never Give Up!" He repeated "Never Give Up" seven times, and that was the end of his speech. The audience responded with thunderous applause.

Actually, the applause given him was not as much for his speech, but for his life which knows not how to give up. Churchill was born prematurely in the eighth month of pregnancy. He had a speech impediment as a child and was last in his class. Because of his large physique and jolly disposition, he was misunderstood as arrogant and conceited. In his primary school records he is stated as being "a hopeless child". In secondary school, he was kept back in his class 3 years. Eventually, he was unable to enter Cambridge or Oxford and matriculated in the Military Academy. Even for the Military Academy, he flunked the exams twice before he passed, and he lost in his first elections when he entered the world of politics, which then he worked as a journalist before he tried again and was elected. Churchill, who spent 21 years in Parliament for the Labour Party, and was a leader in social reform, had failed so many more times than he succeeded, that he once registered as a member of the conservative party when he ran for office, but still had lost.

Nonetheless, just like in his commencement speech, he overcame his speech impediment, even won the Nobel Prize in Literature, and became a hero during wartime and a great politician because he never, never, never gave up.

The biggest crisis for Churchill was during WWII. He was the Prime Minister at the time, and during a speech at Parliament he said, "I have nothing to offer but blood, toil, tears and sweat." And in another speech he declared, "We shall not flag or fail. We shall fight on the beaches, we shall fight on the landing-grounds, we shall fight in the fields and in the streets, we shall fight in the hills. We shall never surrender."

Churchill was a hero who did not give up, and because of this he was able to reverse the tide of war and lead the Allies to victory.

Happiness Guide

Pessimists see only the difficulties even if an opportunity comes their way. Optimists see an opportunity every time they meet difficulties. Suffering is a chance for growth. Don't conclude that you have tried every possibility, but rather have hope and courage and give another try. There will still be another opportunity.

I can do it

1. I will see the hidden grace behind the suffering and I won't fear it. Crisis is a true opportunity and through failure I can succeed.
2. Even if I have lost everything, I will not give up. I will have the courage to give another try. There is always a silver lining.
3. I will always believe in a good outcome and drive forth with assurance. A promised future is for the one who never gives up.

Don't Quit

When things go wrong, as they sometimes will,
When the road you're trudging seems all up hill,
When the funds are low, and the debts are high,
And you want to smile, but you have to sigh,
When care is pressing you down a bit,
Rest if you must, but don't you quit.

Life is queer with its twists and turns,
As everyone of us sometimes learns,
And many failures turn about,
When he might have won had he stuck it out.
Don't give up though the pace seems slow,
You may succeed with another blow.

Often the goal is nearer than
It seems to a faint and faltering man;
Often the struggler has given up
When he might have captured the victor's cup,
And he learned too late, when the night slipped down,
How close he was to the golden crown.

Success is failure turned inside out,
The silverlint of the clouds of doubt,
And you never can tell how close you are,
It may be near when it seems so far,
So stick to the fight when you're hardest hit,
It's when things seem worse,
That you must not quit.

– Unknown writer

18 *Be a Well-wisher*

CONSIDERATION

You, so precious   It was when I was launching my magazine. I wished to find a way to share heart-warming anecdotes with multitudes of people, and I concluded that publishing a magazine would be the best way. But people opposed the idea, saying it would only consume money; that it would be like throwing water on thirsty soil. Since I am a person who doesn't consider loss when dealing with worthwhile projects, I stuck to my opinion and took action.

However, I couldn't think of a compelling name for the magazine. I even opened a contest with a one million won prize(about 1,000 dollars) for the right name, but none fit my taste. Then one morning at dawn, just as I awoke from my sleep, the name came to me: "You, So Precious!"

'You, So Precious? Sounds good.'

That instant I'd felt a warm embrace. Unexpectedly, tears streamed down my face. Yes, I am special, you are special, everybody is special.

There was no reason to worry anymore. This is how You, So Special was created. Many people have rediscovered how special they are through this magazine, and they convey messages of thanks, saying they have had the blessing of discovering special people around them they hadn't known about before.

Some time afterwards, I realized through a short poem written by Mother Teresa, that she was the embodiment of 'You, So Special' spirit. You, the reader, are one of the persons referred to in this poem.

Only One Person at a Time

I never look at the masses as my responsibility.
I look at the individual.
I can love only one person at a time.
I can feed only one person at a time.

Just one, one, one.

So you begin , I begin.

I picked up one person

maybe if I didn't pick up that one person

I wouldn't have picked up 42,000.

Same thing for you, [⋯]

just begin.

one, one, one.

Throw your remaining shoe out the window   Gandhi barely made it onto a departing train. That instant, he dropped one of his shoes on the platform, but he couldn't retrieve his shoe because the train was already moving. Thus, Gandhi took off his other shoe and tossed it next to the fallen one. One of the people accompanying Gandhi, startled, asked Gandhi why he had done this.

Gandhi smiled and said, "Imagine a poor fellow finding an odd shoe on the ground. This shoe would be useless to him. However, now he will have the other pair."

Let's try to follow Gandhi's example.

THE BLESSING OF GIVING

Bill Gates and Warren Buffet, who rank as the 1st and 2nd wealthiest men in the world, know just how they should spend their money.

Bill Gates announced that he plans to leave his executive position in two years in order to devote more of his time in bettering medical and educational situations around the world.

Meanwhile, Warren Buffet donated 37 billion dollars, which amounts to 85% of his whole fortune, to Bill Gates' foundation and to other various foundations. The United States press reported this to be the largest sum to ever be donated to charity.

These two men differ in their contributing methods, but they have one thing in common. They both believe they must return the money they have earned back to society.

The story does not end here. After Gates and Buffet announced their intentions, more and more people have been adding their share to the culture of giving.

The philosophy of giving When you give, it is proof of your existence. Elizabeth Bibesco said, "Blessed are those who can give without remembering and take without forget-ting." Like so, giving is the greatest blessing for both the giver and the receiver.

Andrew Carnegie was someone who valued money, not as an end, but as a means of social improvement. Among his famous quotes is, "The man who dies rich dies in disgrace." He became a man of great wealth with his steel business, but instead of bequeathing his wealth to his family, he gave it all back to society. The money he left behind amounted to a grand 500 million dollars. With the money he provided, hun-dreds of museums, libraries, art galleries have been built under his name, not to mention the notable Carnegie Mellon University in Pittsburgh.

Though he was called the Steel King, he had one of the warmest hearts and his philosophy of giving is something we today should learn.

A HEARTWARMING STORY

A beautiful strike-out   Here is a touching story from the history of professional baseball.

Larry Doby was the first African-American to be accepted

into the major leagues. In 1947, he played his first major league game for the Cleveland Indians. Thirty-thousand people watched with interest at the first black man to play on the field, and radio listeners around the nation listened with high hopes. However, when Doby was up to bat he got so nervous he got three consecutive strikes. Doby, feeling ashamed, dejectedly went to the dugout and hung his head.

What moved the crowd came after that. The most powerful hitter at the time, Joe Gordan was the next player up to bat. He'd hit a foul ball, but never had he received three strikes. But this day, Gordan went up to bat and struck out. It was preposterous! Gordan trudged back and sat down next to Doby and hung his head just like Doby. Gordan had consoled his

teammate by showing Doby that even a great hitter could get struck out.

After this incident, the two became buddies and they stayed close friends long afterward. The walls between black and white, rookie and veteran, professional and amateur can be easily demolished by encouraging and cheering on one another.

A very special night out   The following story appears in How to Be a Winner and In fluence Anybody by James Merritt.

In order to eat out, your mother has to clothe me, shave my face, brush my teeth, comb my hair, put me in my wheelchair and take me down the porch steps, open the car door and put me in the car, fold the pedals on my wheelchair, lift me up and adjust me in the car seat, fold the wheelchair and put it in the trunk, walk to the other side of the car and drive to the restaurant. She has to get out of the car and unfold my wheelchair, open the car door to turn and lift me, put me back in the wheelchair, put out the foot pedals, close the car door and lock it, push me in my wheelchair into the restaurant, and put the pedals back up so that I'm not uncomfortable. Then, while we eat, your mother has to feed me, pay for the food after we finish eating, and push me outside, and she has to do the same thing all over again. And when all this is over, your mother tells me in a truly sincere voice, "Thank you for a wonderful evening, dear."

Even during her husband's last days, the wife in this story continues to show her love and devotion to him and makes him feel genuinely alive.

Do you wish to live the way God intended? Then, jump over the border and into a life of sharing and giving.

Happiness Guide

Everyone is a precious person. There is no wrong in seeking grace. Miracles come when you spread words of blessing and good deeds. Become someone who offers blessings and good deeds to others. You have so many things to offer. Good deeds will come back to you like a boomerang.

◀€ I can do it

1. I will check my blessings. I am special. Nothing in the world is as precious and blessed as life.
2. I will become a distributor of blessings. My good deeds will bear miracles.
3. I will share what I value the most with others. Anything that stays still will rot, but sharing will multiply the joy.

Boomerang of Good Deeds

The result of a good deed will go round and round until it eventually comes back to you.

One day, a young man was on his way home from the city when he saw a car on the side of the road that had broken down. He pulled up to the car to see what was the matter. The battery had died. The young man went to a nearby farm, borrowed some cables and connected it to his car's battery to help start the dead one. The other person thanked him and tried to hand him a reward for his services, but the youth declined and instead told him to help someone out when he found a person in need.

About two weeks later, the young man's father was driving home from an auction that had been held in a neighboring town when he got a flat tire. The elderly father wasn't strong enough to change the tire himself. Just then, a car pulled up and a man got out. This man changed the tire for the elderly man. The old man was so grateful that he wanted to reward him with some money, but the other driver declined. "About two weeks ago, I had a similar incident and a young man helped me out. He told me I could pay him back by helping someone else in need instead of giving him the money."

This is the law of nature. Good deeds will come back to you like a boomerang. This is also a promise that Jesus made:

"Give to others, and God will give to you. Indeed, you will receive a full measure, a generous helping, poured into your hands all that you can hold. The measure you use for others is the one that God will use for you." (Luke 6:38)

VII

Blessing of the Rainbow

Laws work everywhere and principles are solid.
Just satisfy those conditions and it will come true.
Use the principle of hope, the principle of total improvement,
and the Rainbow principle(aka "Blessing of the Rainbow")
to train yourself.

19 *Blessing of the Rainbow, Where All Goes Well*

SOMETHING VERY FEASIBLE

Mother and daughter   There are households where things just work out for them.

This is the conclusion I have come to after meeting numerous people. There is a mother and daughter who have reaffirmed this belief for me.

I've only met the mother on a couple of occasions, but with the few meetings that we've had she left a very strong impression. Every word she speaks is full of life's wisdom. She was sincere and giving. Each time we met, she never came empty handed.

I met her daughter, Dr. K, while I was studying abroad.

Since I was acquainted with Dr. K's then husband-to-be, I had the honor of being the officiator at their wedding ceremony. Dr. K is also a sagacious and earnest person, and I've come to trust her due to her drive and persistence. She has now become one of the top landscape architects in Korea.

I recently met Dr. K and we talked about our current lives. As we talked, I realized that all her siblings are doing well in society. Her eldest brother returned to Korea after a professorship in the States, and was working as a professor at a leading university when he was scouted as CEO for a company. And her second brother is a prominent figure in the sports world.

Dr. K lent a hand for the landscaping and roof construction of my research institute. We were short of funds near the end of construction, which is when she pitched in, so our circumstances didn't allow us to pay her for her troubles, but still Dr. K showed thorough responsibility by inspecting the construction progress from morning till late at night. The outcome of her work was so deeply imbued with an expert's hand that we all exclaimed with contentment.

There is no doubt that there are "good households"; decent families, customs and histories.

Right now, I try overlapping images of the mother and

daughter in my mind. I already knew by intuition that the off-spring of that mother would do well. This is because she shared the habits of those who succeed.

There is a principle, a fundamental truth, to success. This mother and daughter are people who practice the seven Blessings of the Rainbow which will be recapitulated in the following pages.

A nearsighted boy   This is from a short essay which appears in Stories from My Heart by Fr. John Powell.

I cannot forget a boy who was afflicted with severe myopia. He could only discern what was right in front of his face. Because of his condition, he learned to interpret the world the way he saw it.

When the teacher at school wrote something on the black-board, he determined it was because the teacher wanted to write down the things she had to say to the class so she wouldn't forget. Why were road signs put up so high where people couldn't even read what was written on them? The boy guessed it was so bus drivers could read the signs and inform the passengers where they were headed.

Baseball games were the hardest to comprehend. He got up to bat and could distinguish the ball only at the moment it

whizzed past home plate. He didn't have enough time to swing at it, so he didn't see anything fun about baseball.

One day, he went to see an ophthalmologist. The doctor chose a pair of lenses that were just right for him, and then the doctor told the boy to take a look out the window. For the first time in his life, the boy saw the expressions on people's faces as they walked by. He could even see the leaves on a tall tree. He saw the sky and the clouds. It was amazing!

The boy told me his experience and he told me it was the second most exciting thing which had happened to him in his life.

"Then what is the most exciting thing that happened to you?" I asked.

The boy gave me a dubious look as if to say, 'Isn't it obvious?' But I didn't know.

"The most exciting day of my life was when I realized Jesus loves me and that He has an intention for everything that happens to me in my life."

I hope that the readers of this book experience something as exciting as this.

One, I hope that you gain the wisdom to look afar like the boy who found the perfect lenses for his eyes.

Two, I hope your eyes open to the fact that you are loved and your life is full of God's meaning.

You will have these two exciting realizations in no time once you practice the Blessings presented in this book.

BLESSING OF THE RAINBOW

You can change   For the past 100 years, brain experts believed that neurons in the human brain stopped growing and formed a stabilized structure at the age of three. This means the human cerebral capacity is determined at infancy, just like fate.

However, there was a study which flipped this theory

upside-down. Professors Elizabeth Gould and Charles Gross at Princeton University published a paper in the journal, Science, with the title, "Neurogenesis in the Neocortex of Adult Primates" on October 15, 1999.

They made an astonishing announcement that new neurons continue to increase in adult primates. Also, that new neurons which are created in the deep center of the brain don't stay only in that area, but spread out to various areas of the cerebral cortex which executes such functions as reflection, decision-making, and learning.

Although the research was conducted on primates, Dr. Gross concludes as thus, "There is no doubt similar things occur in humans because primates and humans are fundamentally alike."

This experiment suggests that certain areas in the human cerebral cortex are transformed to become new variations everyday. In other words, people can change with persistent training.

If I tell people, "Change your life with the Blessing of the Rainbow," some people may counter,

"How can that work? Nothing's changed up till now."

Now, the answer's clear: "It will change."

Monkeys changed. Why can't humans?

Structure of the "Rainbow Principle"

You have already seen a general outline of the "Rainbow Principle" at the beginning of this book. You have also studied each principle in detail. Now let's have a full review of the principles once more.

The "Blessing of the Rainbow" or the "Rainbow Principle" consists of seven guideposts(i.e. "Blessings") for a successful life, and they touch on all aspects from intellectual and emotional to determination and resolve.

Intelligence Development (With All Your Strength: Left Brain)	Blessing of the Rainbow 1 **Think Positively** Blessing of the Rainbow 2 **Scatter the Seed of Wisdom**
Emotional Development (With All Your Heart: Right Brain)	Blessing of the Rainbow 3 **Nurture a dream** Blessing of the Rainbow 4 **Believe in Achieving**
Will Development (With All Your Soul: Corpus Callosum)	Blessing of the Rainbow 5 **Discipline Your Language** Blessing of the Rainbow 6 **Discipline Your Habits**
Personalizing (Repeat: Overall Personality)	Blessing of the Rainbow 7 **Never Give Up**

As I have mentioned before, the Blessing of the Rainbow is a systemized principle taken from the Jewish success principles of the Talmud and Shema Yisrael. This principle also matches what brain researchers are telling us today about the human cerebral make-up.

Two of the Blessings concern the Left Brain, and are about intelligence development, which corresponds to Shema Yisrael's "with all your strength".

Another two of the Blessings concern the Right Brain, and help development of emotion in correspondence to Shema Yisrael's "with all your heart".

The Corpus Callosum is related to Shema Yisrael's "with all your soul" and two of the Blessings discuss this in terms of developing will power.

Lastly, in relation to overall personality is a Blessing which corresponds to Shema Yisrael's instruction to "repeat" all which have been mentioned above.

ENDLESS CHALLENGE

Absolute optimism, absolute hope   It was a couple of months ago. A twenty-five-year-old Protestant youth living in Gwangju telephoned me asking for a consultation.

The employee who answered the phone connected him to me because he was in such a mentally unstable condition that she was unable to calm him. He told her that he thought he was going crazy, that he wanted to die; he was in the depths of despair. At this critical moment, when he was grasping at loose straws, he happened to come across a showing of my television lecture of "All Goes Well-Blessing of the Rainbow," and thought I was the one who could help him.

For half an hour I listened to his plight and it was this:

"Father, my dream was to study the flute in college and become a great flutist, but I've already been rejected five times from universities in Seoul. I always do bad on the college entrance exams. This is my 6th try, and since the past years have been full of frustration, the burden of this exam weighs heavier and heavier as the days near. I don't think I can live if I don't make it this time. I've already wasted five years⋯. Everyday is full of dread. What should I do?"

I felt that this fellow was someone who needed the 1st Blessing of the Rainbow; 'Think positively.' I gave him two pieces of advice.

"First, look at your life in the long run. Five years out of your whole life is not such a long period of time. Second, don't despair. Always think positively, always have hope! Your time is sure to come."

I offered these words of hope and ended my message with, "Halleluiah! Amen!" and blessed him in the name of the Lord.

Surprisingly, within two weeks, the youth called again. This time he called to tell me he had been accepted from a university. In the lad's exulted voice I discovered yet another rainbow.

The reason the youth could pass the test was because he had accepted "absolute optimism, absolute hope!" as his own. This positive way of thinking gave him confidence for his exam and released him from his fear from failing yet another time, and it made him have assurance that his faith and prayers will be answered.

It's the same for anybody. We must have the conviction to declare "I will think positively no matter what! I will have hope no matter what!"

Let's believe in love regardless how desperate the situation is. This love will echo endlessly inside us and will ring true in our hearts, "Absolute optimism! Absolute hope!"

Life is long and possibilities are endless   Einstein, who was recognized as the world's greatest scientist was asked by a class of students, "Sir, why do you keep learning when you already know so much?"

Einstein answered, "If the area in this circle is the amount of knowledge I already have, the area outside of the circle is the unknown. The larger the circle grows, so does its circumference, which means the area which is in contact with the unknown also increases. Right now, my circle is larger than yours, which means the area that touches the unknown is greater than yours. So you can see, there are more things I don't know than you. How can I idle away?"

We can't do anything about the past. The important thing begins now. The time we can control is the present and the future. Everything depends on what you will make of your future. Bear in mind that you have more time than you may think. Everything depends on the way you look at it.

Practice, practice, practice   Itzhak Perlman who was born in 1946 in Israel, crossed the Atlantic to become a famous violinist. He said, "I am playing the violin, that's all I know, nothing else, no education, no nothing. You just practice every day."

What would practice define to a person who started playing the violin at the age of four? The amount of practice alone is not the answer. It is how detailed the practice is the quantity plus the quality. In other words, to become an expert you must practice by engraving each note into your head like you are carving each note into a piece of oak.

During his whole life, the one thing Itzhak Perlman emphasized to his students was practice. It might seem trifling, but to a musician nothing is as important as practice. There was a special rule when he had his students practice, which he'd attained from Rivka Goldgart, his own original teacher, and that was to practice slowly in keeping with the beat. He said there were students who complained they never got better no matter how much time they invested into practicing. When he asked such cases to show him how they had practiced, nine out of ten, the odds were they had practiced at a tempo that was too fast.

The reason why fast playing doesn't work is because of

how the brain functions when repeating a subtle note. For instance, like when learning the complex passages of N. Paganini, the brain must have a distinct and detailed input of the information. However, when a violinist plays the music in a swift vigor and practices this way, precise information cannot be stored in the brain, and thus precise information can't be delivered to the fingers. That is why he told his students to practice at a slow tempo.

This is not just for music. The same goes for scholastic studies or anything else. If you want to be a true master at what you do, you must be prepared to set a goal and invest your time in it. Only practice will make you an expert.

Autobiography in Five Short Chapters

I. I walk down the street. There is a deep hole in the sidewalk
   I fall in. I am lost··· I am helpless.
   It isn't my fault. It takes me forever to find a way out.

II. I walk down the same street. There is a deep hole in the
    sidewalk.
    I pretend I don't see it. I fall in again.
    I can't believe I am in the same place
    But, it isn't my fault.
    It still takes a long time to get out.

III. I walk down the same street. There is a deep hole in the
     sidewalk.
     I see it is there. I still fall in··· it's a habit.
     My eyes are open I know where I am.
     It is my fault.
     I get out immediately.

IV. I walk down the same street. There is a deep hole in the
    sidewalk.
    I walk around it.

V. I walk down another street.

– Portia Nelson

20 *Be Happy Now*

THIS IS HEAVEN

Someone who knows joy   Being in the presence of this person makes me feel good. Her voice is invigorating and she's always smiling, giving joy to the people around her. She is the novelist Young Ahn. She wrote a series of articles from January 2005 to March 2007 for my monthly magazine, ⟨You, So Precious⟩.

Young Ahn calls herself a "small wild flower". Now, after retirement, she lives for the service of others, for God. I had the opportunity of writing a recommendation letter for her book, Dreaming of the Heavens. Here is what I wrote:

"Young Ahn's disposition is as lovely as her voice. Everywhere she goes, whomever she meets, whatever she sees she emanates love. After losing her husband several years ago, she raised her three children by herself into essential persons of society. After she sent her children off into the world, she focused her complete love to the Lord and now it seems her life is full to the brim with happiness.

Every time I encounter Young Ahn, I feel as if my soul has been cleansed. She is exceedingly frugal when it comes to her own needs, but ever so generous to others. She is a highly learned person, yet accepts the word of the Lord with the untainted mind of a child. She always looks at the world with an optimistic view and speaks of hope with a mind which is fresh like the green sprouts of a seedling.

If an essay is a work of literature which is written from the heart, this compilation of essays succeeds to convey the distinct tones of Young Ahn's mind. I believe everyone who reads this will be blessed with a refreshed soul as I was."

Young Ahn lost her parents early in life during the Korean War, and even today she does not live in material bounty like many others, but she lives in happiness. This is because she is equipped with "happiness skills," which will be further discussed in this chapter, and entrusts herself completely to God.

Time spent on happiness

How much do people laugh in their lifetime?

Supposing a person lives to be 70-years-old, generally the time spent sleeping amounts to a total of 23 years, 2 years for brushing one's teeth and washing, 26 years working, 1 year for going to the toilet, 1.5 years looking at the mirror, 6 years in a car, 3 years waiting for someone, 2.5 years reading the newspaper, and 4 years watching TV. Then how much time do we spend laughing? About 1-2 years?

Don't be surprised. On the assumption that a person laughs 10 times a day, which only amounts to 5 minutes per day, ultimately the amount of time spent laughing comes to a mere total of 80 days during a lifetime. To be more precise, if a single laugh is calculated as a few seconds, the total amount of time a person laughs in a lifetime only amounts to about 40 days. As you can see, the time spent on happiness in our lives is very short.

How often do you laugh? Are you living a life of happiness?

A bright face will bring a bright future

A first impression is very important. It is said that a person's first impression is decided within 3 seconds.

Albert Mehrabian, professor of Psychology in UCLA, conducted an interesting study on first impressions. His study showed that the elements we use in communication were as follows: language(i.e. content of speech) 7%, visual effects like looks/facial expression/attitude 55%, and auditory effects like voice 38% . These results were most accurate in the case of first encounters.

If his study is applied to smiles and/or laughter, a person's smiling face and sound of laughter determines 93% of a first impression.

Daniel McNeill wrote in his best selling book, The Face, that judges in court seem as if they are being absolutely fair in their judgment, but infact give lighter sentences to a smiling defendant. So, even in court, which should be the epitome of objectivity and logic, smiles and laughter can be your best attorney.

HERE AND NOW

Everything is in my hands   There is a legend about a fisherman named Salim who lived on the banks of the Ganges River.

One night, Salim was returning home, eyelids drooping, after he had completed a day of rigorous labor, and he thought, 'What would I do if I were rich?' That moment, he happened to stumble upon a leather pouch full of small stones. He started to toss the stones into the river one by one while he imagined of riches.

"I'm going to live in a big house."

Tossing another stone into the water, he said, "I'm going to have servants and eat rich foods." He kept throwing the stones into the river until only one was left. As Salim turned the stone in his hand he noticed it glisten in the moonlight. It was then that he realized the stones were valuable jewels.

Salim had been throwing away the riches he already had in his hands while he dreamed of imaginary wealth. Just like Salim, we already have everything we need to make our lives full; we only need to open our eyes to see this.

John Powell, a famous Catholic spiritual activist, claims he has this sentence written beneath his mirror and reads it every time he takes a look in the mirror:

"You're looking at the person who is responsible for today's happiness."

Now is the time to be happy   Poet Hyeon-jong Jeong depicts his remorse over losing happiness in this poem:

Every Moment was a Flower in Bloom

At times I regret
that time back then
could have been a windfall⋯.
that person,
that object
could have been my riches⋯.

Perhaps I should have
dug deeper,
talked longer,
listened harder,
loved more.

Perhaps I let go
half deaf,
half mute;
unconscious⋯.
Perhaps I should have
loved that moment harder⋯.

Every moment was
a flower in bloom.
A flower to blossom
if I'd tried harder.

A happy person does not live for the future. They live in the "now". "Here" is your place of happiness. "Here and now" refers to our daily lives. The ordinary things we experience everyday are all opportunities of happiness. You will never have joy if you go looking for joy someplace else and shrug off your daily life as something dull.

Let's not forget. Your 'today' is the "total settlements" of our entire past and a "security" for your future. You can either kill or save your past and future according to how you live your today.

LAW OF HAPPINESS

Serve others   One day a patient who was suffering from depression went to see Austrian psycho-analyst Alfred Adler. Adler took a close examination of the patient but could not find the root of her illness. After much contemplation, Adler prescribed the patient with a light dose of antidepressants and added, "There is something you must do along with taking this medication. From now until the end of two weeks, everyday you must keep your mind on, 'How can I make others happy?' and devote yourself to this task."

Immediately, the patient went looking for ways to help others and devoted herself to volunteer work, just as the doctor had instructed. A few days into her new lifestyle, the patient felt a wave of immense happiness sweep over her. Like Adler prescribed, just two weeks after she had started volunteering she was free from depression.

Volunteering is a wonderful cure for people in today's world, for those who are worn out or have lost meaning in their lives. Serving others is to serve oneself. You can find happiness with just a little bit of effort.

Live in harmony   There was a father whose five children had all graduated from college and were thus married with their own children. He grew ill one day and he decided to gather his children and sons-and-daughters-in-law together. The children expected he had called to give them their inheritance.

"I've fallen in debt raising you kids and running my business. The debt accumulated and accumulated and now I owe about 700 thousand dollars. I'm not well and now I don't have the ability to make any more money, so each of you must pay off a little of my debt on my behalf. Take these pieces of paper and write down how much you can spare."

His children, who had thought their father had a bit of fortune to leave them, looked at one another dumbfounded. The third son wasn't as well off as the others, but he wrote "50 thousand dollars" and handed it to his father. Reluctantly, the others wrote, "10 thousand," "15 thousand," "20 thousand," and "25 thousand" as if they were bidding prices in an auction.

Several months later, the father called his children home once more, and this is what he said:

"I settled my possessions just in case you children might fight over your inheritance and get into a feud after I'm gone. I will give each of you three times the amount you wrote down last time. This is all I will give you for your inheritance."

At their father's words, the children who had written smaller amounts turned white with alarm.

What comes first? Fortune or life? Inheritance or brotherly love? The answers are simply, 'life' and 'brotherly love'.

Life's joy is as simple as these answers. To go on a journey with a good companion; true happiness is best when shared with others.

Love   You will find happiness when you love someone or something. Love makes anything possible and it completes everything. Emmet Fox, a spiritual thinker, whose preaching surpasses his own time, wrote about the mightiness of love.

Golden Gate of Paradise

Love is by far the most important thing of all.

It is the Golden Gate of Paradise.

Pray for the understanding of love, and meditate upon it daily.

It casts out fear.

It is the fulfilling of the Law.

It covers a multitude of sins.

Love is absolutely invincible.

There is no difficulty that enough love will not conquer;

no disease that enough love will not heal;

no door that enough love will not open;

no gulf that enough love will not bridge;

no wall that enough love will not throw down;

no sin that enough love will not redeem.

It makes no difference how deeply seated may be the trouble,

how hopeless the outlook, how muddled the tangle, how great the mistake;

a sufficient realization of love will dissolve it all.

If only you could love enough you would be the happiest and most powerful being in the world.

So many questions can be answered, meanings and goals be found in love. Love is the beginning and the end. Let's fill our lives with love. This is the key to the happiness you are seeking.

Happiness Guide

Happiness is relative and subjective. You already have everything you need in your hands to make your life rich. Your happiness is determined by how you perceive your situation and the attitude in which you face it. You must find your happiness Here and Now.

I can do it

1. Laugh. Once I laugh, I will feel better, and once I feel better, I will have brighter thoughts. A smiling face and the sound of laughter give better first impressions.
2. I will try things worthwhile; volunteering and serving others. This is the secret to happiness.
3. I will post this on my mirror, "You're looking at the person who is responsible for today's happiness," and read it every time I look in the mirror. I have the key to happiness.

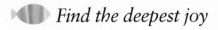 *Find the deepest joy*

It is said that the most fragrant perfume of the rose is begotten from the roses of the Balkan Mountain Range. The highest quality oils are produced from roses which are picked during the coldest and darkest hour of the day at 2 o'clock in the morning. It's because this is the hour when the roses emit their deepest and thickest aroma.

If you are in your life's coldest winter or if you are going through the darkest tunnel, don't despair, but find your happiness within yourself. Because when you do, your happiness will be as blissful as the most fragrant roses from the Balkan Mountains. Remember, it is the joy ripened during anguish which is the deepest kind of happiness.

21 *Be Grateful for Everything*

CELEBRATING GRATITUDE

Thank you and Congratulations   I have the formula which will lead Korea into its "30 thousand dollar era". It's nothing other than "thank you" and "congratulations".

I am certain our country can raise the national income per capita to 30 thousand dollars if only we establish "thank you" and "congratulations" in our everyday language.

I didn't hear phrases such as "thank you" or "congratulations" when I was growing up. At the time, those kinds of expressions weren't used as common language, but as the English language began to have more substantial influence on the Korean lifestyle, our people became accustomed to using "thank you" and "sorry" in our speech. Along with this altered mentality came enormous economic growth. I personally think it is due to our changed consciousness that we could arrive at the threshold of 20 thousand dollars per capita income.

However, there is still one expression Koreans have yet to learn. It is "congratulations".

While I was studying in Austria, I experienced culture shock when I discovered "gratulieren(congratulation)" to be a commonly used expression. They use this locution whenever something good has happened to someone. They even remark "zum wohl(cheers; to your health)" when someone sneezes. This is much like the English version; "bless you."

When I was at Boston University as an exchange student, there was a professor who always asked the students to "challenge me." He loved to challenge the students with effusive questions, but when a student had a correct answer he would didn't fail to recognize their feat with, "Congratulations!"

I believe it is possible to arrive at a 20 thousand dollar GNP through competition, but getting to 30 thousand is impossible without the sense of companionship and the will to congratulate one another.

There are outdated Korean aphorisms such as, "A cousin buys land and you get a stomachache." These sayings must be eliminated from common use in order for Korea to climb a step higher into an improved future.

Thank you, prison cell

Alexander Solzhenitsyn was indicted on forged document charges by the USSR government and declared guilty. He was then sent to prison camp in Siberia and spent 11 years of his life there. The prisoners suffered from unimaginable torture every day, and Solzhenitsyn also had to endure the abhorrent conditions. However, he met Jesus Christ while he was in the prison camp. This changed his life. Later, after Solzhenitsyn was released, he published The Gulag Archipelago, a three volume literary work, revealing the horrors of the Soviet prison camps and their systems. He was awarded the Nobel Prize in Literature for it. In the book Solzhenitsyn discloses that he thanked the prisoncell.

Even the prison could be viewed as something to be grateful for if he tried.

There lived a poor mother and son in Virginia. The father was a clergyman, but had died early on and the mother had to earn her son's tuition by washing other people's laundry and getting cleaning jobs. The son was always grateful for his mother's hard work, and with much effort, he graduated from Princeton University with honors. At the commencement ceremony, he received the honors award and delivered a speech.

He went up to the podium and said, "Thank you mother. I owe my graduation to you. This award shouldn't be for me, but for my mother."

Then, he pinned the gold medal on his shabbily dressed mother. Everyone in the auditorium was moved.

Later, he went on to become a lawyer and professor and eventually became the 28th President of the United States. He was an idealist who received the Nobel Peace Prize. He was Woodrow Wilson.

To be thankful and to know how to express gratitude is a life of beauty.

Dynamics Of "Thank You"

Be grateful while you work   Colin Powell was the first African American to become Secretary of State for the U.S. government. He grew up in a poor neighborhood in New York and worked for a while at a factory. One day, he and the other workers were assigned to dig ditches. One of the men, instead of digging, stood leaning on his shovel and complained that the workers weren't paid enough. Meanwhile, another man kept digging without a word.

Some years later, Powell went back to work part-time for the plant and he found the person who had neglected his work and complained about their wages still doing the same thing, but the ardent worker was driving a forklift.

Many years after that, Powell went to the plant again, and the man who had been lamenting over his work had become ill from unknown causes and had lost his job. The hard working man, on the other hand, had become president of the company.

Colin Powell claims he learned a great lesson through this.

Gratitude; an impetus for miracles   Takeda, the major stockholder of over 100 corporations, also runs the Takeda Pastries, which is famous for its "Tamago Bolo" cookies.

In actuality, it is in these small Tamago Bolo cookies that Takeda's administration philosophy lies.

First of all, Takeda stood by his stance to use fertilized eggs in the cookie recipe, eggs which cost three times as much as regular eggs.

"It's quite remarkable. I kept using those eggs and before I knew it those cookies were reaping in money."

His firm principle to use only the best quality captivated the customers' palates and finally exceeded 60% of market shares.

Recently, Takeda started to implement another new strategy to maintain the high quality of Tamago Bolos. His strategy was for the factory workers to say "thank you" to the cookies.

This may sound preposterous, but an experiment was conducted about the dynamics of positive and negative speech. The breaths emitted from people in anger were collected into a plastic bag, and mosquitoes were put into the bag. Those

mosquitoes died within a few minutes. However, in the breaths emitted from people who were smiling brightly, the mosquitoes survived much longer. This is where Takeda found his new strategy.

"Following the current trend of consumer preference for quality materials used in food, will come a time when people demand a high degree of happiness from the people who make the food. This is because the psychological energy of the maker is passed onto the food that they make." Furthermore, he said, "Try saying, 'Thank you,' three times a day. Your life will change."

Takeda was right. Sales have skyrocketed.

These days, Takeda plays a cassette tape in his factory that repeats, "Thank you. Thank you," 24 hours a day. As a result, each cookie receives 100 "thank yous" before it's shipped out.(Kotaro Hisui, Motto Therapy; Finding Happiness in 3Seconds)

FIND GRATITUDE FOR THE LITTLE THINGS

Unconditionally   Poet Chan-gyeong Seong presents the method of thanking in her poem, "He Gives Me Grace".

He gives me grace.

Curious is the way he gives it;

sometimes as if unsympathetic,

inconspicuous, the way he bestows it.

Sometimes he gives me drops of dew,

sometimes the manna from heaven,

and in the night,

the middle of the night,

he keeps me awake and

like a ray of light

illuminates upon me a radiant verse.

No matter what, no matter what

I implored to Him.

He must have noticed my pathetic pleas,

because no matter how much, how much

I was knocked about

I pretended to be thankful.

Whether it was truth or show,

with leisure or in desperation,

immediately he sees my inner core. He knows it all.

It's rather relieving to know.

Simply strip naked and beseech, because

He will give.

He gives me grace.

No matter how much we are knocked about, let's just try acting like we are thankful. Don't think of anything else or make excuses: just be thankful. The best prayer we can offer is to simply say thanks.

To others   I took close note of an interview with print-maker Chulsoo Lee by a certain broadcasting station. The artist Lee told how he had received much help from a Reverend Lee in his time of troubles. Chul-soo Lee expressed how grateful he was toward the reverend and the reverend said, "You received from me, but pay back your debts to another. To some other person in need."

This is the cycle of gratitude. The best way to show thanks is to do as I have been treated.

Gratitude doesn't end when you repay the person who did you a favor; you have to go a step further in the form of help-ing a third party.

Blessing of the Rainbow has already been printed over 100times, and the people who have read the first editions send messages of amazing change they have experienced in themselves and their neighbors. They also send words of thanks to me and this is what I tell them, "If this book has changed you, now offer this gift of change to your neighbor. This is how you can reciprocate your gratitude towards me."

If you have been moved by this book, then offer it to someone close to you. Your fruit of happiness will augment the more you share it with others.

There is a saying, "You learn as you teach."

In helping someone out, you will try to describe a certain concept and you'll find you need a better comprehension of the idea and that you need to internalize the concept as your

own. To say you really know something means you have to be able to pass it onto someone else and that person has to be able to accept that knowledge into their lives and apply it into their livelihood.

There is no doubt we will catch the rainbow if we integrate the Blessing of the Rainbow into our own lives and share the Blessings with others until we are all infused with those blessings.

Blessing of the Rainbow is an alternative campaign. It's a movement for attitude reform which will lead our people to become the most promising people in the world.

Franklin D. Roosevelt said, "One thing is sure. We have to do something. We have to do the best we know how at the moment. If it doesn't turn out right, we can modify it as we go along."

Let's practice the Blessing of the Rainbow in our lives and pass it on to others. If you do this, you will be empowered to become whatever you want. Your dream will be sure to come true.

Happiness Guide

A person who knows how to be thankful, how to voice their thanks, lives a beautiful life. You will find things to be grateful for as much as you return kindness. The truth is we come into this world empty-handed and we leave with empty hands, and in this way we've been given everything. You have to always bear with you a sense of gratitude and do your best at the task you are given. Gratitude brings success and guarantees happiness.

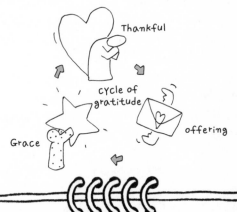

◄≡ I can do it

1. I will say "thank you" and "congratulations". Gratitude brings good fortune.
2. I will be thankful for the little things. There are surprisingly many things to be thankful for in our lives.
3. I will share my blessings. It's important to repay a good deed to the person who bestowed it, but it is more important to pass it on to someone else.

To Always Be Grateful

If my teenage offspring shows me attitude
it means my child is safe at home and not wandering on the streets.
If I have taxes I have to pay it means I have a job to go to
If I have too much to clean up after a party
it means I've spent a great time with my friends.
If my clothes are too snug
it means I have much to eat and my life is plentiful.
If the only parking spot left is in the farthest corner in the parking lot
it means I can not only walk but I also have a car.
If I paid a lot for heating it means I live in a warm house.
If the lady sitting behind me at church annoys me with her poor singing
it means I am able to hear.
If my whole body aches with fatigue it means I have worked hard.
If I woke up at dawn to the irritating noise of an alarm clock
it means I am alive.
And if I get too much email
it means a lot of people out there are thinking of me.
There is so much discontent
and so many complaints that have grown inside me unwittingly,
that when seen from a different angle are all things to be grateful for.

– Unknown writer

The writer is offering a secret solution to bring the Korean GNP to the 30thousand dollar level. His advice is biting: we have to go beyond competition and holding one another in check and must spread a culture of symbiosis. In other words, we must open an era of "congratulations".

– Byeong-du Son(President of Seogang University)

This book utilizes various stories to distinguish what the contrasting 2% is for individuals who are successful and happy compared to other ordinary people. The strength of this book is that rather than being a theoretical, educational book it is a practical happiness guidebook that can be used in the real, intense world.

– Byeong-young Ahn(Yonsei University professor)

Blessing of the Rainbow, just like the title, is a warm and beautiful guidebook that instills us with dreams and hope, wisdom and courage. If we open our ears to the concrete happiness and success theories that were intently researched by a pastor who wishes to spread the world with happiness, soon enough we will be choosing bright, optimistic thoughts and positive behavior.

I anticipate for this book, as the "Korean Talmud," to be especially loved by young mothers who are devoted to their children's educations.

– Hae-in Lee(Catholic nun and poet)

This book is very unique and interesting. The author, finds numerous episodes from worldly goings on. He also finds light, clever rules to happiness which are blended in our everyday lives and by finding these things he, like the poems of Wordsworth, makes our hearts flutter with the colors of the rainbow.

With that in mind, Fr. Cha Dong-yeob is a mysterious alchemist.

– In-ho Choi(novelist)

I'd always lived in poverty because I had a mentality of "just a little more, just a little more."

It came as a relief when the book told me to say "thank you" three thousand times a day.

Of course… I already have so many things to be grateful for.

I'm much obliged to this book for making me realize this.

– Jeong-min Hwang(KBS announcer)